William MacGillivray
A Hebridean Naturalist's Journal
1817 - 1818

Edited by Dr Robert Ralph

The publishers extend their appreciation to the University of Aberdeen
for permission to publish this journal.

The publishers acknowledge subsidy from the Scottish Arts Council
towards the publication of this volume.

The publishers are also grateful for the financial assistance from:
Mr Jonathan Bulmer, The North Harris Estate
Mr Andrew Miller Mundy
Dr Robert Ralph
Dr David Horrobin
Ms Tessa Tennant
Mr Andrew St. John, Glenalmond Tweed Company
Mr A. M. Pelham Burn

The publishers are particularly grateful to Dr Robert Ralph as editor, to Peigi MacLennan for
keying in the transcript and to Bill Lawson for his contribution to the publication.

Permission to reproduce the colour plates of MacGillivray's paintings courtesy of
The Trustees of The Natural History Museum, London.
Permission to reproduce William Bald's Map of Harris, 1804-5 courtesy of
The Trustees of The National Library of Scotland.

First published in Scotland in 1996 by Acair Ltd., 7 James Street, Stornoway, Isle of Lewis.

Design by Acair
Printed by Stornoway Gazette
Cover photograph by James Smith.

ISBN 0 86152 122 6 (Paper Back)
ISBN 0 86152 127 7 (Hard Back)

Contents

Foreword

William MacGillivray was born in Old Aberdeen on 25 January 1796. His start in life was not a particularly well favoured one. His father, also William, was from the Outer Isles and was a student at Aberdeen University; his mother was a local girl, Anne Wishart, and nothing is known of her. They were not married. Soon after William's birth his father joined the Cameron Highlanders and served in the Peninsular Wars. There are conflicting accounts of his fate, some say he was killed at the Battle of Corunna in 1809, others give a later date for his death, but when the young William was three years old he was taken to his uncle's farm at Northton in Harris and was brought up there. He went to the village school at Obbe, and in his early teens came back to Aberdeen, finished his schooling and then went to the university where he took an MA degree. MacGillivray developed an interest in natural history at an early age, in all its aspects, in botany, geology, zoology, and ornithology but after his first degree he began to study medicine, although he never completed his degree in the subject. In the summer of 1817, aged 21, he decided to go home to Northton.

MacGillivray never wrote an autobiography but he wrote a number of journals or diaries. Sadly, most of these were destroyed in a library fire in Australia at the end of the last century, but two survived. They are now in the care of the Special Collections Department of Aberdeen University Library. They were given to the University in 1934 by Mr William Lachlan MacGillivray of Eoligarry House in Barra, a nephew of William MacGillivray. It is the first of these journals that is published here, the journal that he kept during twelve months at Northton in 1817-18, a year in which MacGillivray was deciding on the course of the rest of his life.

Editorial Note

I have been a lecturer in the Zoology Department at Aberdeen University for nearly thirty years, and for the last six I have been curator of the Department's museum. Soon after becoming the curator I realised that the collection had been established by William MacGillivray in the 1840s. I became fascinated by the man, by his many talents, his capacity for hard work and the the sheer quantity of his work, and his obsession with accuracy and the truth. I was also aware of the injustice of his name being almost unknown in his native land when he should be recognised as Scotland's finest naturalist. In collecting material for a biography of MacGillivray I became aware of two journals in the Special Collections Department of the Aberdeen University Library. The first of them is published here, while the second, written a year later in 1819, describes a remarkable walk from Aberdeen to London, to see the bird collections in the British Museum.

The journal as it is printed here is substantially the same as the original and I have retained MacGillivray's punctuation, use of capitals and spelling of place names. Where I have felt a note of explanation is needed I have added it in brackets or in a footnote, but some words have defeated me, for example, I have no idea what a grishkin is. If any reader can enlighten me I would be glad to know. MacGillivray recorded all of the animals and plants that he saw using their scientific Latin names but I have changed all of these to their English equivalents. As a dedicated field naturalist and observer MacGillivray kept detailed lists of the plants and the animals that he saw; I have removed these from the main text into Appendix I. This journal was written at a time when bird taxonomy was in its infancy. The only book that MacGillivray had to help him identify birds was Linnaeus's Systema Naturae, a book written in Latin with very limited descriptions of a small number of species, and of course, he was working before binoculars became available, his only identification aid was his gun. Throughout the journal MacGillivray refers to "examining" and "describing" a specimen, of plant or bird. Examining in this sense means making a detailed comparison of a plant species for example, with the published description, the number of petals, sepals, and other anatomical features. He also made detailed descriptions of bird specimens that he collected. These included precise measurements of bill length, wing length, foot length, the number of wing primary feathers, and plumage colour. The descriptions, made at this stage in his life, were an important training for him, in bird anatomy and in the methods of scientific species description, both of which were to play a major role in his later career as an ornithologist. However, they are of very limited interest in a publication of this nature and I have not included them here.

I am especially grateful to Ian Callaghan, of Scarista House in Harris, for his interest and enthusiasm in MacGillivray without which this journal would not have been published. Bill Lawson, of the Old School House, Northton, has an unrivalled knowledge of the place names and genealogy of the Western Isles and I am pleased to acknowledge his help in providing Appendix II and the family trees; they have added greatly to the value and interest of the journal. I also have to acknowledge the permission of the Aberdeen University Librarian to publish the journal and the staff of Acair for their help and enthusiasm, especially Peigi MacLennan, who undertook the arduous task of transcribing the words from MacGillivray's quill to electronic disc.

Dr Robert Ralph,
Zoology Department,
Aberdeen University.

April 1996

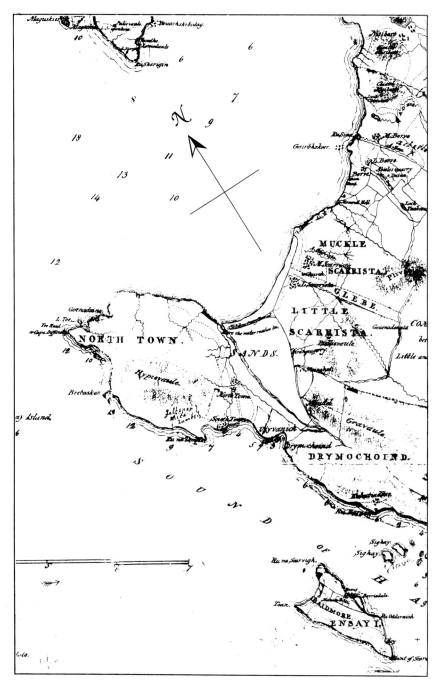

Map of Harris, by William Bald, 1804-5

Journal
of
a year's residence
and travels
in
The Hebrides

by

William MacGillivray

From 3rd August 1817
to 13th August 1818

Old Aberdeen, Sunday 3rd August, 1817.

I am again determined for a tour through part of the Highlands and Isles. In regard to my motives - the principal one is connected with the article pecunia but it would be doing injustice to my favourite study, not to say that Natural History also put in its vote for the expedition. Mr James Shand (a student friend), actuated by a desire of extending his knowledge in Topography and Zoology, intends to accompany me. He has already made his departure, but will meet me tomorrow at Kemnay. My baggage will be heavy: but I submit with cheerfulness to any temporary inconvenience, when it becomes the mean of procuring permanent benefit. I may here with propriety enough give an account in detail of my accoutrements: In the first place. My clothes differ in nothing from those commonly worn. I take some changes of femoralia and pectoralia, (breeches and shirts) linnen, stockings, and two pair of shoes. My hat is just like those of my neighbours, without the vast umbelliform brim, which characterises the physical or Linnoan cut! (After Linnaeus, the Swedish taxonomist*). For my studies and amusements by the way, I take the first part of the First and the Third Volume of the Systema Natura; Smith's Compendium Flora Britannica; Campbell's Pleasures of Hope; drawing paper, pencils, paints & crayons; paper, ink and pens; one pound of gun-powder, six pounds of shot, flints and bullets, powderhorn & fowling-piece, hair-line and hooks and a quarter of a pound of snuff. The other articles which can scarcely be reduced to any distinct class are the following: pocket compass, knife, soap, razors, silk-thread, wax, buttons, sharping stone, needles, lancets, opium, a flute & some small boxes. All, excepting my gun, packed into two bundles, clapped upon my shoulders, after the manner of a knapsack. The objects in view are: money to be obtained from some of my friends to enable me to prosecute my studies, my improvement in Natural History, particularly in Ornithology, Ichthyology and Mineralogy: Botany too - inurement to hardship, the habit of early rising, dexterity in the use of the gun, proficiency in physiognomy (judging character and disposition from a person's external features). Knowledge of men and manners, romantic ideas, practical imagery, sketches of landscape drawings in Zoology or

---

* Linnaeus's Systema Natura, written in Latin, was the only readily available text dealing with zoological classification and Smith's Compendium was a botanical guide. Pleasures of Hope was a long poem written by Thomas Campbell, first published in Edinburgh in 1799. Its subject was the consolation that Hope provides when in situations of danger and distress. It was enormously popular in its day, a runaway best seller that ran to several editions.

Botany - improvement in taste, some patience, resolution and inflexibility. If I catch rightly at opportunities, I have a fair chance of accomplishing all these ends. Objects more particularly in view are, an interview with my uncle, the collection of shells and birds and plants, a knowledge of the syphilis insontium and specimens of the Itch insect.* I am all in confusion. It is the necessary consequence of the procrastination which makes so prominent a feature in my real character. It shall be given up however, and that immediately. I have been at Dr Barclay's (one of MacGillivray's medical lecturers) and received his instructions relative to subjects of enquiry.

Fochabers, Morayshire Tuesday 5th August

I left Old Aberdeen yester morning at a quarter from six o'clock. Mr Craigie who had assisted in packing my portables accompanied me as far as the canal bridge at Kittybrewster. I reached Kemnay between nine and ten. It is situated on the Don above Inverury. Mr Shand met me on the way, and conducted me to the house of the Rev Dr Mitchell, minister of Kemnay. Here I breakfasted. This gentleman's family consists of his wife, three sons, and a daughter. The sons are Robert, Patrick and William, the daughter Nancy - of the former the first is a surgeon, and said to be a very studious and perhaps clever gentleman, the second is a student of law, the third follows the farming occupation. The young lady, in as far as I may judge is not possessed of any brilliant qualification. The whole group indeed are much tinged with rusticity. Before twelve we took our leave of this family, crossed the Don at the Miln of Kemnay and ascended Ben-o-chith, (Benachie) the highest hill in this country. From the summit we had a fine view of the circumjacent country, and of the sea near Aberdeen. It is situated about twenty miles from Aberdeen. I observed no plants upon it which are not to be found in much less elevated situations. The Round-leaved Wintergreen grows among the masses of rock upon the southern side of the hill, near the summit. The top is rocky, and particularly encircled with two decayed walls, very thick, but composed of small stones. I have not yet learned by whom it was so fortified - on descending we entered the ruinous castle of Harthill, to the uppermost apartments of which we ascended by the stairs which are still in

---

* Itch insect. There are several small organisms that this might refer to. The most likely is *Sarcoptes scabius*, the scabies mite. It is a microscopic organism that burrows under the skin and causes an intense itching and an eczema-like condition.

good order. It appeared to have been destroyed by fire. The Small Bur Parsley, Common Wild Chamomile, Great Nettle, Common Chickweed, Common Feverfew, and some grasses grew in the apartments; and the chimneys appeared to have been lately occupied by Swallows and Jackdaws. It is composed of a central oblong building, terminated at either end by a circular tower. Leaving this, we regained the highway, on which we proceeded to Mill of Williamston, where we passed the night. The family here consists of Mr Stephen, a silly, good-natured, rigidly religious fellow, his wife, no brilliant personage, his son James, a middle aged farmer, & his daughter, a thirty three year old rustic wench. There were two excise officers here, illiterate unmannerly, bulky fellows - MacNaughton and Watt, the latter, a coarse brute, told us in his bragging humour, that he had studied Divinity both in Edinburgh and London, though he confessed he was no master of the ceremonies. This night passed very disagreeably. Next morning we got up about seven and breakfasted about nine. We then proceeded on our journey, passing over the hill of Foudland, where there are slate quarries. The slate here is said to be superior to that of Eisdale in Argyllshire, which is the best of the western counties. In crossing a heath between this and Huntly we shot a plover. I had before this today shot a small bird unexamined and yesterday two linnets. We reached Huntly, a country town of no great beauty situated on the Bogie river, there we got some refreshment in a Mr Robinson's of Mr Shand's acquaintance. Huntly is 38 miles from Aberdeen, and 20 from Banff. About six we arrived at Keith, another small and rather mean country town, where we drank tea and set off for Fochabers where we arrived about nine o'clock rather fatigued. Yesterday I travelled 35 miles, the distance, however, from Aberdeen by the turnpike road is only 26. Today our journey was 31 miles. The country over which we have passed, including all the space from Aberdeen to Fochabers, is composed of large but low hills, generally smooth on the surface and covered with short heath, and between these well-cultivated plains and gentle declivities. The heaths consist principally of the Common Heath, Common Ling, Mat-grass, Heath Rush, and Common Crow-berry. Several hill berries and grasses too are common on them, and a few other plants, the Small Upright St. John's-wort, Eye-bright, and Broad-leaved Wall Hawkweed.

The plants which I observed in our yesterdays course were only such as are found in the vicinity of Aberdeen with the exception of the Common Golden-rod, Red Bear-berry, and some berries found on Benochi, (Benachie) one of which I take to be the Cloud-berry.

(At this point in his journal MacGillivray produced a long list of plants seen during the day. The list is of around 85 plant species, recorded by their Latin names, and is reproduced in Appendix I with their common English names. See Appendix I: The plants seen between the Glens of Foudland and Fochabers, during a walk of 35 miles).

The plants under cultivation seen today are Oats, Barley, Wheat, Turnip, Ryegrass, Soft Broom-grass, Purple Clover, Sea-kale, Potato, and Flax. Of the Soft Broom-grass we saw only one field. The plantations, which are pretty umerous, particularly between Aberdeen and Huntly consist of the Scotch Fir, and of natural wood we saw only a few patches near Huntly. They were composed entirely of the White Birch.

The birds seen are the Red Kite, Woodpigeon, Carrion Crow, Pied Wagtail, Red Grouse, Corn Bunting, Partridge, Skylark, Meadow Pipit, Magpie, Kestrel, Yellowhammer, Jackdaw, and Golden Plover.

The only Quadruped (wild one) we observed was the Brown Hare. After supper we wrote into our Journals, examined some plantage, birds, and drank some Whisky Toddy.

Wednesday, 6th, August. after 9.A.M.

It was nearly eight before we got up. The liquor we drank last night left us rather heavy: but we were otherwise well, and free from the crippling effects of travelling upon hard roads & in warm weather. I have forgot, by the bye, to mention the state of the weather, This I shall however regularly note in future. On Monday we had a good deal of rain, the sky was thickly clouded, & it blew briskly. Yesterday, the skies lowered in the morning, but after ten we had an excellent day.

Forres, 8 at night.

We reached Elgin at the distance of 9 miles from Fochabers, without the recurrence of any adverse circumstance. Here we scrutinized the ruins of the Cathedral, which had been a very fine Gothic pile. The Chapter house is still nearly entire, as is the grand entrance. The other parts though much is standing, are quickly falling into ruin. To prevent this in some measure, masons are at present employed in securing the remaining parts.

The country through which we passed is flat and not very well cultivated. The road passes through a large fir wood belonging to the Duke of Gordon. In it I found some funguses which I was obliged to leave without examination. On leaving the Cathedral we paid the man who kept the key eighteen pence and passed through the town of Elgin, a mean, little, country town. It was crowded with people, this being a market day. In a large fir wood near Elgin I saw the Coal Tit and Treecreeper. Nothing else very worthy of recording occurred till we reached Forres at half past six. The heaths of Murray shire differ from those of Aberdeen in containing considerable quantities of Gorse and Common Juniper. Excepting some oak in the wood near Elgin all the plantations consist of the Scotch Fir.

(At this point MacGillivray included another long list of plants. See Appendix I: The plants seen between Fochabers and Forres).

The birds seen were the same as those of yesterday, excepting the Red grouse and Partridge, and adding the Hedge Sparrow, Hobby, Common Tern, Coal Tit and Treecreeper.

As we were coming out of Elgin, we were accosted by a poor man who said he had been turned off by his laird, and was travelling to Aberdeen. I gave him a shilling, observing that it was not in my power to give more. 'Oh! Lord bless you! you have given too much,' replied the poor man. On the heath about half way between Elgin and Forres, we fell in with a flock of plovers, among which we both fired, and killed three. To day we have travelled only twenty one miles. Since I left Aberdeen I have examined (examined in this sense means to make a detailed comparison of the plants with his botanical textbook) the Wood Vetch, Common Quaking-grass, Pellitory of the Wall, and the Corn Marigold. The Pellitory was found by the wall of Elgin Cathedral.

Inverness, 7th August, 1817

We slept so long this morning that we did not get away from Forres till after breakfast. Forres is a small, mean town, like all which we have seen since we left Aberdeen. Near the bridge laid across the Findhorn river we were accosted by a drunk fellow, who told us he had been fifteen years in a Dragoon regiment, and had been discharged for some defect in his sight: observing our fowling pieces, he took occasion to speak of his own dexterity in the use of the musket, wagering 'two bawbees' that he would fire ten shots in a minute. We found it difficult to get rid of him, which we were anxious to do, as he looked exceedingly blackguardish. We at

14

length however accomplished our end. Soon after a troop of women and children came up with comical dresses, and carrying burdens. They and the fellow just spoken of joined some of their companions at the other end of the bridge. As the Dragoon pensioner had been inquisitive about our country and destination, we thought it prudent to charge our pieces, Mr Shand his with three pistol bullets, and I mine with a large and a small one. We learned soon after that they had taken the upper road to Nairn, so we took the lower, not aware that the two roads join about three miles from town. Near Nairn we passed this Tinker crew, and could not help admiring the fluency of speech and harmonious pronunciation of the little imps.

The country to the North of Forres is flat, and very well cultivated. The plants are the same as those found all along with the addition of the Broad Bean. Wheat is common, as well as the Barley-bear. Toward Nairn the country appears rather barren, and is much less cultivated. On the heaths is a good proportion of Gorse. The soil of Murray Shire is very light, being in common brownish earth containing gravel, sometimes clayey, upon a base of gravel or sea sand. The country rises gradually from the sea shore which is sandy. Woods of fir are frequent, and some of them very extensive.

Passing through Nairn a small town, nine miles from Forres, and nineteen from Inverness, we proceeded over a flat, barren uninteresting country. The highland mountains were now in view, but none appeared of any considerable elevation. We got to Inverness in good time, and entering in style proceeded to Geddes's Hotel where we took up our lodging. Wild plants are numerous in the country through which we have passed today, as appears from the following list, containing those which I observed by the road side in flower. (See Appendix I: The plants seen between Forres and Inverness).

Birds seen today were the same as yesterday, but exceedingly few.

Saturday, 9th August, 9 A.M.

Yesterday, we took it into our heads to visit the Fall of Foyers, said to be eighteen miles distant, and left town about 10 minutes after 11am. For some miles from town the road is very pleasant, passing through plantations, and commanding at intervals beautiful views of the river Ness and surrounding country. On the north bank of the river, and about a mile distant from town stands a hill thinly covered with trees, which has been compared to a ship with its keel uppermost. It is quite different in structure from the neighbouring hills and were it not of very considerable size might be deemed artificial. It is called Tom na h' iurich. After walking very briskly for an hour we came to a wood which obstructed our view of the river. This wood continued till we were within a mile of the eastern extremity of Loch Ness. We had an excellent view from the road. The lake is very long and narrow, lying nearly east and west. On either side are hills rapidly sloping, and well wooded from the middle to the waters edge. On the Northern side, is a peculiarly beautiful hill sloping uniformly, and streaked with the beds of torrents. The upper end of the lake and the inclosing hills were enveloped in clouds. None of the distant hills seemed to rise to any considerable elevation: but the white mist resting on their summits added much to their apparent altitude and gave a peculiar charm to the scene. The pleasure which a distant scene affords when partially involved in obscurity arises from fancy. When all is limited and defined, the eye soon comprehends the whole. Hence I am of opinion that in landscapes of the first order something should always be left for the fancy to enlarge or beautify. We reached the banks of the lake at twenty minutes from one. We had travelled so quickly that, besides being drenched with perspired matter, our hands had become oedematous and stiff. The sultriness of the day had been the chief cause of this. In this part of our course, the plants I observed were much the same as those noted on the 7th. The plantations consisted chiefly of Fir. For some miles up the lake, on the south side, the road passes through natural woods of the White Birch and Common Hazel, with the Common Oak and Hawthorn interspersed. Farther on the hills become rocky, and often precipitous, with immense blocks along their side. Here the White Birch alone grows - about fifteen miles from Inverness we came to a deep valley, through which a stream passes. A bridge over this stream appeared so romantic that we took a sketch of it. The rain had come on by this time. After finishing our sketch we proceeded up the glen. The scenery was sublime. Two very deep ravines, separated by an almost perpendicular rock of vast height, and bounded by precipitous hills covered with birch, and other trees. I have seen grander scenes but the grandeur here was blended with beauty, and the sullen silence that prevailed was scarcely interrupted by the falls of the rivulet that ran beneath our feet. Had I been alone, the wildest ideas had rushed to my mind. Here we met some natives who informed us that the fall was still three miles distant. So we travelled onward through the woods, till we came to an Inn where we got Tea - as we were excessively hungry, we laid up a good store, and then proceeded to the Fall of Foyers. The scenery here is the most romantic imaginable. The rain fell in torrents, and the river was, in consequence, much swelled. From a very contracted channel cut deep into the solid rock, it bursts almost perpendicularly down widening as it descends, one continued sheet of foam. Below, it dashes with such force upon the rocks, that a great part is resolved into thick vapour, and is squirted into the air to a great height; from which circumstance the fall is named by the natives Eas na smuidadh, the Cataract of mist. The lower part, through which the river again bursts in a hundred foaming cataracts, is composed of vast masses of rock, which had been precipitated from the surrounding cliffs, during the continuance of that convulsion which gave a bed to the torrents for I hold the notion absurd that all rivers have formed their own channels. The inclosing rocks are dark coloured, and almost perpendicular, thinly wooded along their faces, and jutting into promontories overhanging the torrent. These promontories afford as many excellent views of the fall, which is such that it cannot be all seen from any one point. The Scotch Fir, White Birch & Common Ash grow upon the brinks and along the precipices - The Wood Vetch I saw in two places - and found the Alpine Saw-wort on the brink of one of the rocks. In the place in which the latter was found, the condensed vapour fell in such quantity, that I, who went nearer the precipice than Mr Shand, was in a moment drenched most pitilessly. The water fell from my hat, and coat tails literally in cataracts. The surrounding scenery partakes of this wildness. Above the fall, the river forces its way through a rocky channel inclosed by rugged hills, and below proceeds through a deep wooded valley to Loch Ness. At a quarter after eight we left the fall, and retraced our former footsteps in darkness, through a wild country, over deep roads, and in a continued pour of rain. We reached Inverness about one o'clock. The length of this day's journey may be about 38 miles, or perhaps a little more. I was not much fatigued, but the cuticle was rubbed from my thighs and legs in many places. Mr Shand was more skinned than I, and had got a blister on his foot.

Muir of Ord.

Today we were up before nine. The weather being still bad we didn't leave Inverness till 12 o'clock.

(At this point in the journal MacGillivray made a list of the plants he saw. See

Appendix I: The plants found on the south side of Loch Ness).

The animals we saw were but few in number. The Hobby, Kestrel, the former on a blasted tree, the other at the Fall, Chaffinch, Meadow Pipit, Crossbill, a grey slug, a frog, and a toad. No high-bounding son of the mountain appeared to remind me of the days of Ossian, son of the years of other times, or of Fingal King of men.

The lake did not appear to me to be more than three quarters of a mile in breadth. The North banks appeared less diversified, and covered with wood. One bay, and a ruinous castle on promontory near it formed all the deviation from this uniformity which I observed.

After leaving Inverness we travelled along the south side of Loch Beauly, the termination of the Murray Firth through a country neither agreeable than otherwise. The rain continued so as to prevent me from noting the plants which occurred. They appeared to be the same as those found in Murray and Nairn shires. The Great Water Plantain was the only additional one: it grew in ditches & marshes very plentifully. We went to view the Falls of Kilmorack near Beauly. The river crammed into a very narrow channel, between perpendicular, but not very high rocks, bursts suddenly into a wide expanse. Growing still broader as it descends, it falls in broken streams over a ledge of rocks, and again bursts away. The trees in the neighbourhood are principally Birch. Some men were fishing in the eddies below the stream. The view of this afforded me considerable pleasure, more especially as this fall is of a totally different nature from that which I had lately seen. In the latter all was wild and grand; in this there was much of beauty intermixed with grandeur. We proceeded to Beauly a small collection of houses situated at the head of the Frith. Here we bought some biscuit for the mountains. We were so fatigued that we could not proceed farther than this place where there is a small Inn, at which we put up, and comforted ourselves with a good fire a most substantial supper and a glass of reeking Toddy. Mr Shand's blister increased so much today as to cripple him. For my own part I was much fatigued.

The Yellow Bird's-nest was found in a wood upon the banks of Loch Ness. It was first observed by Mr Shand.

Sunday, 10th August.

We arrived here last night, as has already been said and refreshed ourselves with

18

an excellent supper, and a long and sound sleep. I believe I am getting into better condition with regard to muscularity than I was in when I left Aberdeen, as to Mr Shand, whether he be growing stouter or not I can not say. But this I know, that he has looked these two days as if he were half-drowned, and so in fact he was. Today after breakfasting I read some passages of the Pleasures of Hope, and a chapter or two of the Book of Job, which book, by the way, I like very much, perhaps better than any other in the Old Testament. About 12 o'clock, I began to draw the piece of mountain scenery which I had sketched on Friday. Mr Shand was similarly occupied. At this we continued till night, without finishing. The weather today has been partly foul and partly fair: but it being Sunday we didn't care for travelling with our arms and baggage, more especially as we were quartered quite to our satisfaction. This house is the best by far, considering circumstances, that we have fallen in with since we left Aberdeen. For a very excellent supper consisting of mutton, pork, diced beef, eggs, bread & butter, we paid only one shiling cash, and a like sum for each of our meals today. Indeed I wonder, how in such a dear country as this, the people of the house could afford to rate provisions so cheaply. Tomorrow we shall set off early, if circumstances prove favourable.

I shall, now that my companion is snoring full loudly in his bed, note some particulars which have escaped my recollection when writing my notes. In the house in which we lodged at Forres, we were assailed by winged Bugs, of what species I do not know, some of which I caught upon my skin. They did not bite however, or at least not severely, for I did not detect any marks. Mr Shand was so fatigued yesterday, that he would gladly have passed by the Falls of Kilmorack, but my enthusiasm prevented us from falling into such unpardonable negligence. The waiter at Geddes's Hotel at Inverness, where we lodged has published a small volume of Poems dedicated to the Marquis of Huntly. They are most miserable things - as to himself, he is a very genteel looking fellow, and appears to be very clever in his way. Tonight a man of whom I enquired yesterday about Wm MacLachlan's friends came to ask of the maid about me, saying that he thought so much of me as to become interested in my prosperity, and left a rose with her to give me. By the powers, think I to myself, it is a miracle that anybody should think so of me - when my whole life has been nothing else than a series of blunders, follies and crimes, but I trust I shall amend.

Poll-ew, Ross Shire, Tuesday, 12th August.

Yesterday we left Muir of Ord house about Sunrise, and travelled onward to Scatwell on the river Conan, where we breakfasted. Of the plants which I observed in this course, about 8 miles in length, I have only noted the following;

(See Appendix I: The plants seen from Muir of Ord to Scatwell on the river Conan, about 8 miles.).

Leaving Scatwell we forded the river, and proceeded along its Northern banks, leaving the path occasionally to view the fine cascades which it forms. Scatwell is at the extremity of a long valley which may be considered as the termination of that lower part of this division of the highlands termed the Machar, a word used to denote a flat sandy tract of country. So we now entered upon the true or majestic highlands and Eagles and Black Oats now for the first time made their appearance. After travelling along the Conan for about five miles, we followed the Pollewe road over the mountains. I observed the Alpine Saw-wort by the stream mentioned near the place where the Skye and Pollewe roads meet. While travelling the hills, we were occasionally delighted with distant views of some of the loftiest mountains of Ross and Inverness Shires, many of which had patches of snow scattered along their sides. On the farther side of a small lake at a place named Badaleuchi we saw a small wood of pines. On the lake there were flocks of ducks. The road on which we travelled was excessively irregular and hard, so that we had only reached the northern extremity of Loch na sin at eight o'clock. Here we saw two people from Pollewe who were driving cattle. They informed us that the Stornoway packet had sailed in the morning, but would be expected on Wednesday. After giving them a dram and taking one ourselves we set out, under the resolution of sleeping in the hills. Accordingly after proceeding about a mile we began to look for a convenient station, and after some search found one. It was the bed of a torrent situated upon the side of a high valley at the upper end of Loch Mari. We pulled some heather which we put under us, and after eating of some biscuit and beef which we had taken with us addressed ourselves to sleep. But the rain fell in heavy showers, and Mr Shand grew sick and shivered excessively. So after some time, we again fell to pulling heather, with which we made a sort of canopy to protect our heads and shoulders from the rain. It felt exceedingly cold. Mr Shand, who had not been accustomed to hardship or privation, felt the effects of this more than I, who have enjoyed full opportunities of becoming inured to cold and hunger and fatigue. Mr Shand continued shivering, while I fell asleep: nor did I wake till day break, when my companion informed me that he had spent the time very uncomfortably. On looking at our lodgings I found that the Yellow Mountain Saxifrage grew in great abundance around us, a sure proof of the altitude of our situation. As we both felt chilly, we clapped our baggage to our shoulders, and trudged along. At the head of Loch Mari, we forded two rivers which pour their waters into it, and proceeding along the western margin of the Lake. About a mile farther on, the scenery is most sublime. On either side of the lake are very lofty mountains, and at that time their rugged brows were wrapt in mist. Most of them are precipitous in the extreme, scantily wooded along the water's edge, and teeming with a thousand foaming rills. On the western bank is a fine natural forest of pines which extends a considerable way up the hills. I have already hinted that I am partial to the pine in mountain scenery; the view of this wood, in such a situation could not then fail to afford much delight. The road here is the most rugged imaginable; and as we were wearied, and destitute of that refreshment which a comfortable nap affords, our progress was but slow. Mr Shand complained of his blisters; and I, though free of these, & fresher than he, found it impracticable to walk with any tolerable degree of celerity. When near the middle of the lake our curiosity was excited by the noise made by a mountain stream rushing along its bed. On approaching the spot from which the roar proceeded, we were agreeably surprised to find a most beautifully romantic cataract or series of falls. I began to sketch this delightful piece of scenery, but was prevented from finishing it, by the rain which began to fall. So we proceeded along the lake. The rain fell heavily; & we were soon wetted to the skin. Our condition was rendered more distressing by Mr Shand's being unable to march with sufficient quickness. The road near the northern extremity of the lake passes across a high and very rugged hill. On its summit, we betook ourselves to a cave for shelter. As we were sitting here, Mr Shand thought he observed two bright eyes in a dark hole, and was ready to swear he saw the membrana nictitans drawn several times over them. Of course it was a cat, or a marten, or an owl. So we proceeded to load a gun; but I wishing to be sure of the fact, before being at the trouble of cleaning my piece, and afraid that were I to fire, the shot would come back from the rock in my face, began to look with a more discriminating eye - when behold the object of our alarm proved to be a fragment of rock with the water glistening on its surface! We arrived at Pollewe in a woeful plight about 4 o'clock.

I saw the Alpine Saw-wort in several places by the side of Loch Mari and found the White English Stonecrop upon a stone in the water. Eagles have been often seen since we left Scatwell. Today, I tried opium as a stimulant and found it to answer very well. It did not succeed however with Mr Shand, but appears to have induced its sedative effects. For since I began to write these notes, he has been snoring in his bed. Upon my soul! I can't help comparing him to a drowned owl! Comparisons are often involuntary.

One of my favourite studies is physiognomy. I must not neglect to seize every opportunity of cultivating it. Today, I had an excellent opportunity of scrutinizing the features of my companion. He fell asleep in the cave mentioned above, in a semierect or sitting posture, the best possible for my purpose. When one is asleep, at least soundly asleep the features all assume their real bent. Where no restraint can exist, there can be no deception. The result of my scrutiny was, that whatever good qualities he may possess, he appeared to be deficient in generosity. Care, or the desire of gathering, evinced by a peculiarly characteristic flattening and puckering of the chin, and elongation of the lower lip, was the most prominent feature. Some circumstances tend to corroborate this opinion. That shaking of the hands, or sometimes of the whole body, peculiar, I believe, to over careful people, and displayed when collecting or securing any thing that requires some exertion, he possesses in a considerable degree; the other proof is negative yet if not conclusive, is at least roborant. I never heard of any generous action performed by him, never heard himself express a generous wish, never saw him perform a truly disinterested act. He has had numerous opportunities since we left Aberdeen, yet none have been embraced. 1st. a poor highlander, who had been put off by his laird, & reduced to beggary, asked a little assistance to enable him to pursue his journey to Aberdeen. He rendered him none; 2nd a poor cripple fellow at Forres got nothing: 3rd an old strolling Irishman - nothing; 4th a deaf and dumb hero, who met us tonight as we were coming to the Inn would possibly have shared the same fate, had not I proposed giving him sixpence each. To judge very charitably of him then I may say, if he perform a noble action, it must be at the instigation of another. I must confess however that I am no adept in the science: and could wish that I were mistaken in my judgement. There certainly are ways of explaining his conduct in the instances mentioned, without prejudice to his character, and considering my own very numerous defects & failings, I ought to be charitably inclined.

The Highlanders are a most inquisitive set of mortals. When you meet one, he hails you: From whence have you travelled? How far do you go? What news have you? How sold the meal? Is there any price for cattle in the south? Have you got tobacco? & all this is explanable, by the consideration of attingent circumstances, but I dare not enter upon the subject.

Wednesday, 13th August.

It was nine before I got up my feet were a little swelled, my toes practically decorticated, (skinned) and my left knee stiff and painful. In other respects I was well enough. Mr Shand was sick, and the region of his toes presented one continued series of vesications (blisters). He attributes his complaints to a small quantity of opium taken yesterday: but sure it is needless to search for such causes, when more direct and valid ones are to be found. Few people have sufficient strength of mind to own their failings.

Loch Mari is a large lake, about 14 miles in length. Like Loch Ness it is but narrow, particularly for some miles from its upper end, where the breadth is scarcely half a mile. About its middle it begins to form a large bay, which extends for some miles along the west side toward Pollewe. In this bay are several large islands covered with heath & Pine and other trees. The scenery in the neighbourhood is among the grandest I ever beheld. All is wild & savage with scarce a single spot that might be called beautiful. The river which issues from the northern extremity of the lake, though larger than the Dee or Don, has only a course of one mile. Its waters are perfectly clear, as the country about the lake is rocky, with but little earth. The country between this and Inverness is but thinly woody. In the higher or central part between the two seas there is no wood at all, but the moors even there bear evidence of the former existence of very large trees. Most of the hills are only adopted for rearing sheep, and the sheep walks in this neighbourhood are said to be very extensive.

Manse of Kiose, Lewis Island, Ross shire, Saturday 16th A.

On Wednesday night, the packet and two other vessels arrived from Stornoway with Cattle. We spent the evening with a parcel of gentlemen Tacksmen in Lewis, and some Drovers, none of whom I knew excepting Mr Robinson, Collector of Customs. Next day, after breakfast, we embarked in the packet, and after a tolerably pleasant passage, arrived at Stornoway in the dusk. The master John Clark, a fine active little fellow is married to a niece of my Uncle's wife. So as there was no convenience in his own house for us, he procured lodgings, which was done with the greatest difficulty; the good people in the publican line being more accustomed to Bacchanalians than to scamps of our description. On Friday morning we breakfasted in the house of a wright, married to an elder sister of my uncle's wife. They are very agreeable people, and the young couple John Clark and his spouse appeared to enjoy perfect felicity. The girl possesses one of the finest faces I have yet seen. It is composed of mild, modest, sincere traits or features. Here we also dined. About three o'clock, we set out for Kiose. In taking my leave I took advantage of the custom prevalent in the isles, of kissing. The country on our way we found composed of wet flat heath. In the evening we arrived at Kiose. Near the house we fell in with my good friend Sandy, from whom and from his father Mr Simson I got a most hearty welcome. So after shifting (changing our clothes), taking tea and supper, and enjoying a good deal of pleasant conversation, we retired to bed.

This morning I got up about half past six. Mr Shand dozed on till breakfast time. After cramming our paunches, we set out for the moor, with our guns, and a dog belonging to the house. The Red Grouse is very numerous here. We succeeded, but indifferently however, only killing, among us all three, half a dozen. Sandy observed a deer lying in a glen at some distance from us. So I was dispatched in pursuit of him. After a little maneuvring, I got within two hundred yards of him, and had a fine side view; but thinking to get nearer I began to return, when he observed me, and started up. I fired, but made no execution. We regained the house about 4 o'clock dined, drank tea, and supped. I took a stroll with Mr Simson about the farm: we talked on various subjects, and after returning conversed for a considerable time on subjects of natural history. Nothing could exceed the kindness with which we were treated. The utmost attention was paid to Mr Shand, who appeared to some of the family scarcely to merit it. Who is that, that you have brought Doctor? inquired Misses Oona and Margaret of me, he doesn't speak like you - we would take him for a mason. I had apprised Mr Shand of the unsuperable dislike of the Hebrideans to the Scottish dialect. But he made little use of my advice, in fact it is no easy matter to break off a habit. The discourse, in consequence, was but little directed to him. My favourite, Jessy, is not at home. Her brother Charles has gone over to Uig for her. She is to return on Monday night, but before that time, I shall probably be off.

Sunday, 17th August.

Today, it was after nine before I got up. I have done nothing in the physical way since I arrived - but shall commence my studies and observations tomorrow. The weather being bad we did not get out to peripatise. After 12 went to the church, which is situated on a peninsula in the neighbourhood. Mr Simson gave the people a sad scolding for the irregularity of their attendance. His manner is very vehement. Let me now endeavour to delineate his character. Many of the traits are so peculiar and so strongly marked that I cannot fail to hit them. As to his person, he is above the middle size, very robust, and much in the Johnsonian style. His neck is somewhat contracted betwixt his shoulders - his physiognomy is masculine in the first degree but somewhat unpleasing. His manners, though not bearing the mark of a high polish are characteristic of manliness, honour and integrity. His conversation, if not learned, is pleasing and didactic, intermined with some humour. I had formed a rather unjust opinion of him from the description of others, but I found nothing but extreme kindness, the most liberal hospitality, and engaging behaviour. He appears to be devoid of keen sensibility, and formed for a calm and rigid philosopher. On returning from church we dined. Sandy and we went to see a small birch wood near the house - the only piece of natural wood, or rather shrubbery, in the Long Island. After tea, we read a discourse in some philosophico-religious book, and joined in prayer with the minister. To this I had no objections. The evidences historical and internal of the Christian religion, are too strong not to convince an unprejudiced mind of its truth. I had gone astray by framing a system from the observation of nature guided by a self sufficient but fallacious Reason. This system happened to disagree with the maxims inculcated by the religion of Jesus - so I discarded the latter, and adhered to my own. The principal blame of this I have to lay upon Thomas Paine, at least the reading of his works was one of the causes of my infidelity. But I scarcely regret that I have so long wandered in a dubious path, since it has led me to a security of which I had never otherwise been truly conscious. I have been inquisitive about objects of Natural History. Some shells are to be found on the shores. Sandy is to gather them, and either to send or to carry them to Aberdeen for me. Deer are very numerous, and so bold as to come under night, to eat the corn below the house. Some have been shot, within three hundred yards of the house. Though I am no epicure, I cannot but be much gratified with the table part of my entertainment at this house, which may justly be styled, "a Heaven in the midst of Hell," a complimentary nomination bestowed by an Englishman on Applecross. Today we had for breakfast, tea, oat-bread, butter, cheese, eggs and dried salmon; to dinner, Red grouse, potatoes, salmon, curdled milk, and bread; to tea, tea, bread, butter and cheese; to supper, sowans and milk. The hours of diet too appear to be more regularly observed than in most parts of the Hebrides. They are nine, three, five and nine. There are fine lakes in abundance on the moors well stocked with Trout. I intend when in Harris to collect as many species and varieties of fresh water fish as I can. In regard to my conduct during this week, I shall attend most strictly to my morals and studies. I propose to examine at least twenty five plants, and ten animals, and to collect twenty specimens of some kind or other. I shall not devote more than six hours each day to sleep, shall grasp with avidity every opportunity of gaining knowledge, shall endeavour to render myself agreeable to people with whom I may converse, shall guard against intemperance and immorality, and walk humbly with my God. I know by experience that true happiness is only to be earned by strict regularity and propriety of conduct. My experience of good and evil, which in the short time of my past existence has been great, has taught me much, and I shall be much to blame if I do not profit by it.

In regard to the article True Love, my heart, I believe, is now vacant but I expect soon to find a worthy object, with which to occupy it. Love is the most generous of passions, and I long to indulge it. If the girl to whom I allude answer my expectations, my native sensibility will ensure a degree of happiness, which no circumstance may ever entirely destroy: happiness pure, and unsullied by any ungenerous motive. The love which I bore to the once dear Helen gave me no pleasure, but involved me in unutterable anguish. But this, if once fostered, shall be free from the distraction attendant upon despair, shall inspire me with a noble enthusiasm - and make the creaking wheels of life roll with facility. O Fancy! I am much beholden to thee: and though the fairy dreams have often vanished, to leave me in the torments of cruel Reality, yet I shall not cease to cherish thee. When thy cheering smile sheds its radiance on my lonely heart, sorrow flies like the morning mist. Continue to pour thy soothing balm upon the rankling wounds which a capricious fortune has inflicted. The short and uncertain sunshine of pleasure I shall not overcast with the gloomy presages of misfortune. "Man is the proper study of man." Let me begin with my own heart: the scrutiny, even should I fail, will lead to advantage.

Monday, 18th August

I rose today about half past seven. Mr Shand dosed on till ten. Accompanied by my friend Sandy, I strolled about the house, noting the plants in flower. They are the following:

Self-heal	Common Wild Chamomile
Succory-leaved Hawkweed	Common Yarrow
Common Ragwort	Red Bartsia
Sneeze-wort	Yellow Rattle
White Trefoil	Eyebright
Common Yellow Bedstraw	Common Daisy
Common Purple Clover	Narrow-leaved Mouse-eared Chickweed
Curled Dock	Broad-leaved Mouse-eared Chickweed
Tufted Vetch	Sharp-flowered Rush
Common Ling	Great Water Scorpion-grass
Marsh Lousewort	Creeping Crowfoot
Spear Thistle	Corn Spurrey

Those out of flower were the:

Silver-weed	Sea Plantain
Soft Rush	Spotted Palmate Orchid
Hoary Plantain	Common Cotton-grass
Ribwort Plantain	Floating Fox-tail-grass
Common Shepherd's Purse	Sweet Gale
Floating Sweet-grass	Pansy Violet
Yellow Iris	

This morning I examined the Devil's-bit Scabious, Small-flowered Hoary Willow-herb, Sharp-flowered Rush, Mugwort, Common Yellow Cow-wheat, and Field Gentian.

To the list of plants in flower I have to add the:

Upright Bedstraw	Field Gentian

Common Nipple-wort	Red Dead-nettle
Common Yellow Cow-wheat	Small Upright St. John's Wort
Yellow Scorpion Grass	Small-flowered Hoary Willow-herb
Soft Broom Grass	Pansy Violet
Mugwort	

No frogs are found here, or in fact, in any part of the Long Island.

Marig, Harris, Inverness Shire, Tuesday 19th August

We left Kiose yesterday after 12 o'clock. Sandy accompanied us for some way. Previous to our departure I had examined the Capra Hircus (goat), promised to return soon with some drawings for the ladies, and pocketed a quantity of oat bread and goat milk cheese. By a river about two miles from Kiose, on which Mr Simson has a cruive (a fishtrap). I found the Flowering Fern in considerable quantity. We travelled on, passing through a long tract of flat wet muir, without the occurrence of any thing worth noting, till we came to the Harris boundary. It now began to rain, and continued foul till we got to Marig. The last two miles were walked, or rather tumbled through a very rugged part of the country and in darkness. Mr Shand at every fall cursed the country most pitilessly: while I though possibly equally fatigued, bore through with philosophic resignation. Such adventures were perfectly familiar to me. Yet I was galled most severely by an observation made by the fellow, ironically, and aimed at my veracity: viz that this was "famous hebridean fun." The fun, said I, is very good - and so in sooth it was to me. When we arrived we found that part of the family had gone to bed, and after supping, shifting, and warming ourselves at a blazing fire, we followed their example.

Today we got up by nine, breakfasted, and prepared for a fishing expedition. Mr Macleod, Mr Roderick and we rowed to the head of the small bay near the house, where we commenced. On the stream here is a most beautiful fall, which nearly equals that by the side of Loch Mari. In this stream, and in a small lake from which part of its waters come I caught thirty two small trouts. Mr Shand might have had about twenty. We returned to dinner. My companion, probably by way of atoning for what he had said last night, observed that we had got "good fun" today - In the evening Mr Roderick and I went out with guns; but though we got several opportunities, we did not succeed in killing any thing.

The plants which recurred yesterday on the moor were the Common Heath,

Common Ling, Scaly-stalked Club-rush, Long-leaved Sun-dew, Bog Asphodel, White Water-lily, Water Lobelia, and the Marsh Trefoil.. The black or gray oat alone is cultivated in the Lewis. In this Island there are four parishes. Stornoway, Lochs, Barvas and Uig: The ministers of which are Messrs Fraser, Simson, MacRae and Munro. The whole island, excepting a part at the southern extremity is flat, and in general swampy, though on the west coast there is a good deal of sandy soil. Kelp is manufactured upon the shores in considerable quantity. Black cattle is the principal produce. The wild quadrupeds are the Red Deer, Pine Marten, the Grey Seal and perhaps some small mice. As to the other animals, I know little about them. I shall endeavour to learn more about Harris.

The scenery here is wild and sublime. Lofty hills encompass us. Above the rest Cliseim (Clisham) rises in gloomy grandeur. These hills form an immense amphitheatre, in the centre of which is part of Loch Seaforth an arm of the sea.

North-town, Harris. Thursday, 21st August

Yesterday we left Marig after breakfasting heartily. Mr Macleod accompanied us as far as the mouth of the rivulet, on which we fished yesterday. At parting he gave us a true highland clasp, which spoke to my sentient faculty of a heart warm with tenderness. Excepting the grasp of Jessy Simson, last year, I never felt a more endearing one. As to his character I dare not meddle with it. He has his failings. But I may venture to say with the poet he has "a guileless bosom, true to sympathy." So Fare-thee-well, my dear Friend. May the blast of Misfortune fall lightly on thy frame! Long may'st thou enjoy the little comfort which thy station in life may afford! Roderick went about half a mile further with us. So we travelled on toward North-town. On the hills between Marig and Tarbert I saw the Pale Butterwort thinly scattered. Leaving Tarbert, we ascended the hill of Luskentir - from the summit of which we had a partial view of the west coast of the southern division of Harris - a sight peculiarly pleasing to Mr Shand who was tired to the heart of scenes like those which the former part of our journey through the Hebrides presents. On the sand of Luskentir I gathered some shells, and Mr Shand killed a Ring-plover. We called at Nisbost, but Mr Torrie was not at home. At Borve I saw Mr & Mrs Bethune and the boys: At Scarista, a parcel of fellows of my acquaintance. At North-town we were met by Mary MacAskill, alias Mrs McGillivray, who agreeably to custom gave me a kiss, and conducted us to the house. Here I found my uncle: he is recovering from a very severe pleurisy. Mary appears much altered in features, though still the same in manners and disposition. Excepting my spontaneous introduction to Marion McAskill, nothing out of the ordinary course of things occurred, and in due time we retired to rest.

Today I rose about six, and taking my gun upon my shoulder scampered over the hill of Tastir to Southtown. On Tastir I shot two pigeons, and in Southtown and upon Ui fired several shots without success.

Tuesday, 26th, August.

Well may I exclaim with my very good friend Mr Norman McNiel, "I am out of my latitude." For these four days I have almost forgot what I was about. On Friday, Mrs MacGillivray of Pabbay, Donald, my brother, Mr Norman McNiel, Doctor McKinlay and my brother's teacher were here. Norman is still the same good fellow. On Saturday, Mr Shand & I went round Ben Capval. I shot a scart (shag) on the point of Do, and an oyster-catcher in South town: the latter however fell into the sea - On Sunday, Neil Campbell was here. I took a walk with the ladies - and in the evening went with Marion to the fold. Marion is a very fine girl, tall and genteel in her figure, but rather simple and unsuspecting. "Sweet floweret of the rural shade!" full easily might you be "by love's simplicity betray'd, and guileless trust." but blasted be the heart that could harbour a thought inimical to your virtue. Yesterday I went to fish. Roderick Bethune accompanied me. The weather was not favourable, the sun shining clear, and the wind blowing very hard. So we only caught about a score between us, some of these were pretty large. I have got a catarrh, and yesterday experienced a very distressing pain in my breast. It has worn off however.

Today I rose about seven, warmed myself at the kitchen fire, played with Marion, went to the fold, breakfasted, read part of the Pleasures of Hope to Mrs MacG., sat a while with Marion. Then determined to make the best use of the remainder of the day, and accordingly began to write in my journal. I next cleaned the lock of my gun - then examined the shag and the gannet. The latter had been found in a dying state upon the sea. Numbers of them are cast ashore annually in the summer season. The only place in which they breed is the island of St. Kilda yet they are seen in great numbers along the shores at all times of the day. I have not been able to determine whether they retire to the island each night, but am inclined to think many of them do, as I have seen ranks of them in the evening directing their flight westward. They are almost always upon wing, coasting along the bays & creeks, very seldom passing over land, even an isthmus. When they see a fish they plunge after it with amazing rapidity, and on emerging sit for a few minutes upon the water before they renew their efforts. Shags are very common. Vast numbers of them resort to the caves to breed, indeed they take up their night lodgings in them all the year through. The nest is commonly placed on a shelf, sometimes in a hole and is composed of sticks, heather and seaweeds. The eggs are very long of a light blue or milk colour, and three in number.

In the evening my uncle and Mr Shand and I went to South town to fish for Cuddies, the fry of the coal fish. Mrs MacGillivray accompanied us. We killed a considerable number. I had 52, my uncle 45, Mr Shand 12, Mrs MacGillivray 5. This fish affords the islanders a considerable portion of their food, in the harvest season. It is taken in vast quantities with small circular pock nets fastened to long poles. The bait used is the limpet, the time morning and evening. The fry is a very delicate fish, the yearling is coarse, the full grown fish among the most insipid and unpalatable I know.

I examined today also the Corncrake, a nearly full-fledged pullet of which species, my uncle had caught on Sunday morning.

Wednesday, August 27th.

Rose at 6, cleaned my gun, &c. After breakfast, Mr Shand and I went out with our guns, but did not kill anything. I gathered plants, and on returning home examined the Sea-rocket, Sea Radish, and Black Knapweed; all very common in their respective situations.

Monday, September 1st, 1817.

Last Friday, Mr Shand and I went to Ronaval with the intention of collecting mineralogical specimens. At Ob I called upon MacPhaic. Here we saw a ring which had been found last Spring by one of the children while harrowing. It appeared to be of pure gold, was carved on the outer side, and had an inscription on the inner. This inscription neither of us could make out. I offered a guinea for the ring, which they agreed to take, although they said they had refused it to others. On Ronaval, near the summit, we saw two white grouse, at one of which Mr Shand fired without success. We descended by the corrie on the eastern side of the hill, and returned by Loch Languad to Drimafuinnd.

On Saturday I went with Mr Shand to the Blue Cave on Ui, where we got specimens of stalactite. On emerging I went to Ob, accompanied by John MacPhaic. Here I took posession of the ring, which fits the little finger of the left hand exactly. Donald came to North town along with me. It rained heavily, and I was wetted to the skin. This morning at 2 o'clock I went to the sands of South town with the sand-eel fishers - I only killed seven cuddies.

On Sunday the weather was bad. The ladies and I however took two short walks; one to South town and the other to Ui.

Starlings are numerous - gregarious - frequent cattle folds for the sake of the insects found among the dung. They sit on Black Cattle and sheep probably to pick the insects. Breed in cliffs on the sea shore. Eggs bluish white 4-6. The people here never eat them unless the head is pulled off while the bird is yet warm, pretending that it is full of poison.

Are worms ever generated in flesh that is not exposed to the air? If worms be the progeny of flies they cannot be produced under ground, and if they are not, what miserable blunders have poets and holy writers fallen into: I shall enquire concerning this subject.

The only company we have had of late was Master Lachlan Macleod, Minister of Hirta (St. Kilda) - a pleasantish, flattering, weak man - much addicted to drinking, and Mr Degraves, a smart little Englishman who has undertaken to secure the Northtown sands. He appears to be a good chemist and physician, though I suspect his utter ignorance of the Latin language - I have certainly neglected to note many particulars, which it might in time to come afford me pleasure to read - and to prevent such neglect, I shall during this week daily write a few lines.

Tuesday, 2nd September

I am at sunrise scrawling a line or two. It is a cold morning. Mr Shand had got upon his feet to extend a bespasmed member, & left me rather uncomfortably situated. Thought I to myself. I may rise and do something. A Raven croaked at the door - this determined me I shall endeavour to use this day well. My uncle and his wife were speaking of going to Rodell today. Mr Shand and I shall accompany them - perchance I may get a Ptarmigan on the hill of Rodell.

Nine o'clock - I rallied forth about six o'clock with my gun. On the sand I fell in with a small flock of plovers, of which I shot two. An immense congregation of gulls next attracted my attention. I fired at them, but at too great a distance. In returning by Ui I saw several flocks of pigeons, from which I obtained only one specimen. Pigeons are very numerous here. They breed in the caves upon the coast, lay several times, have two at each time. In summer, when no grain is to be found on the fields, they sit upon the grass; which abounds with small snails - these I presume they eat.

Evening.

After breakfast, my uncle, Mr Shand, I and the shepherd set out for Rodell. The shepherd driving a Ram and a wedder, I and Mr Shand mounted upon two horses without saddles, & tied the one to the other's tail. Near Drimafuind my uncle shot two gulls with my gun. After passing the Mill we left Angus in charge of the horses, and crossed the hill of Strond. By the way my uncle broke a horse's thigh bone upon a stone with a blow of his fist. In doing this there is a knack. At Strond we entered Master Lachlan's hut, where we found his wife boiling potatoes. On emerging, we betook ourselves to the house of John MacDiarmid the merchant, my uncle having some necessaries to purchase from him - from thence to his father's house, where we were entertained with some music by his brother who plays on the fiddle with a most furious bow. In these houses I saw two patients, and directed for the one some doses of salts, and for the other a blister (an irritating ointment to raise a blister). At Rodell we met Mr Degraves, who conducted us to his house, and treated us with a drink of porter of his own brewing. It was after sunset before we got in readiness to depart -and ten o'clock before we reached Northtown - By this time our appetite was keen, as we had not tasted meal since breakfast. The people I saw at Rodell were Mr Degraves, his wife and children, and Mr MacLachlan - the only animal new to me, a Brown Bear, one of which Mr Macleod the Laird has got chained in his garden. It is remarkably tame.

Thursday, 4th September

Mr Shand has for some days been waiting the sailing of the packet. My friends here do not think I should set off so soon. I join them in opinion. It would be foolish in one to leave the country now until I should get specimens of all the birds and shells to be found. Besides I have yet to go to Pabbay, & to return to Lewis. Yesterday, the weather was coarse. I occupied myself in the latter part of the day with shaping and sewing a pair of trousers of country cloth. Marion assisted me. We worked on till eleven o'clock. At twelve I had occasion to go to MacPhaic's old habitacle. Here I found Donald with his bagpipes. So we fell a dancing. There were but three couples. One of which was constituted by Miss Marion and myself. About three o'clock we returned. Today I rose about half past seven. With the assistance of Marion I completed my trousers and clapped them on. They are very handsome in good sooth and moreover very comfortable. In the evening, I went to the side of a streamlet, near the house, & read aloud the first part of the Pleasures of Hope.

Friday, 5th September.

Rose today before six. The wind was still southerly and pretty high but the clouds had passed by, and the sun again appeared. After drinking some warm milk I ascended part of the hill, and scampered along a ridge of rocks that run across its side. I returned by the low grounds collecting unexamined plants. Those which I found were the Wild Carrot, Corn Marigold, Spear Thistle, Common Ling, and Long-leaved Sun-dew. On returning I examined these by Smith's Compendium; and added the sheep to my list. Of this most useful animal, there are two varieties in Harris, the black faced and the white. The former is larger & has more wool, and is kept on extensive sheep farms; the other smaller, shorter but finer in the wool and is commonly found with the small tennantry. In the island of St Kilda there is a curious variety: it is very diminutive and dun coloured. Just as I had returned from gathering lugs (lugworms) on the sand I was spoken to by a boy who had been sent from Rodill to desire me to visit a child of John Macleod's (Ioin ma Dhomh'll ruaidh) which had been despaired of. After cleaning my gun, and taking breakfast, I set out. My uncle was not quite of opinion that I should go. His chief reason appeared to be the fear of disobliging Dr McKinlay. I expressed rather inadvertently my sentiments on the subject of opinions, asserting that I did not care a fig for that of any man living. In truth humanity told me that I could not refuse to use every effort to save the life of a fellow reptile. On arriving at Rodell, I found a houseful of old wives consoling the mother under the apprehension of losing her child. It was ten weeks old, had been indisposed for nearly three weeks past, during which time it frequently put its hands to its head, and started violently. Three days ago its complaints had become aggravated. Today in particular it was very ill. It lay moaning with its eyes half open and its belly much swelled, the tongue was white, the pulse rapid, and the urine obstructed. After clearing the house, I administered a dose of calomel and jalap, and bathed him in warm water. After the bath, he appeared invigorated, sucked his nurse, and fell asleep. Some hours after, the calomel operated, and a second dose was administered. After breakfasting, and giving directions regarding the child I accompanied Mrs MacDonald to her house. She wanted one to look to her throat, which felt sore and timid internally. Tormentil decoction had been recommended. Mr MacDonald came in and showed me a very severe laceration with contusion and sanguineous effusion, upon the shinbone. I directed the application of a poultice, as there was a grumous discharge indicating imperfect suppuration. About six o'clock, I began to ascend the hill of Roneval - on its side, I fired at and wounded a raven. The wind blew most violently from the south, so that I ascended without experiencing the least fatigue. When on the summit I searched for ptarmigans without success till dark. I then descended by a long ridge that pointed to Loch na Morchadh. Night fell before I reached the stream that joins the two lakes. As I was tramping along I observed two small twinkling fires at a considerable distance. I approached to within a hundred yards, when it began to blaze most violently. As the fire did not appear to be phospheric I concluded it had been kindled by sheep stealers, and in consequence declined approaching it. I crossed the stream, and approached nearer on the opposite bank, on which I stood for some time. It then disappeared suddenly, leaving me under the impression of its belonging to some supernatural entities. Then I betook me to my heels and ran very hard, over a piece of moor very rough and swampy and in darkness for two miles till I reached Inis-shi, when I thought me out of danger. I did not slacken my pace here however, but ran rapidly across the sand, favoured by the wind, which blew most furiously. The number of steps I took was 1050, so this determined the breadth of the sand at that place - making each step four feet it will be found to be 1400 yards. On the opposite side I found Marion MacMillan bound for Inis-shi. On regaining the house, I got supper, drank some warm milk, shifted my pedicles (changed my socks), warmed me by the kitchen fire, succeeded in obtaining about a dozen kisses of all dimensions from Miss Marion, and retired to bed.

Sunday.

Yesterday I got up early, as Mr Shand intended to set off by the packet. We left North town about seven o'clock, and reached Rodell about nine without any other remarkable occurrence than that I shot a water bird by the way. The wind blew so strongly that the packet did not venture out. We breakfasted in John Macleod's. The child continued something better. A little calomel had been administered about seven o'clock. The treatment of yesterday was repeated, and some castor oil mixed with brown sugar was given in the afternoon - After breakfast John went with us to a small lake about a mile from Rodell, in which a very light white substance resembling chalk was found. From a small stream near it John lifted a considerable quantity for me, which he carried to the house. I then got a collection of tunes from John Macdonald, and we set out for Northtown. On the way at MacPhaic's at Ob - when I eat three eggs and some limpets. By the road side I gathered some mineralogical specimens. Dinner was waiting me on my arrival - though by this time it was seven o'clock. So we fell to work. Mr Shand retired to bed, as he had to rise before two, in time to reach the packet which was to sail at four or five next morning. I staid up with my uncle till this time, when we bade farewell to poor Jacob. I then retired to bed, and slept soundly. Today, I rose about nine, breakfasted & prepared for going to church by shaving and dressing myself. Mrs Mac. was indisposed with a severe catarrh. On rising she fainted - yet she joined us. My uncle and she were on horseback. Marion and I crossed the sands on foot. When at Scarista we heard that Mr Bethune was so ill that he could not preach. We went to Borve, however - Here we saw, besides the members of the family, Dr McKinlay, Mr McFarlane, and two of Stewart's children from Luskentir. This McFarlane I was told was one of that family which had so kindly received me last year near Benlomond - but before I was made acquainted with the circumstance he had retired. Mr Bethune spoke to me about his leg. The particulars of his case I shall note afterwards. On our way home I called at Scarista where we were treated with tea by Mrs Campbell, and where I saw a curious case, apparently an abscess in the thorax pointing through the sternum. As the boots I had on were rather small, and galled me in walking - I got the horse from Borve to Northtown. Mrs McG was seated on the croup (rump) the whole way and on part of the sand Miss Marion before me.

Monday.

About one o'clock I set out for Scarista, with my gun on my shoulder and sauntered along the high water mark, gathering shells, of which I found several species. At Scarista I saw the child mentioned yesterday - got my foot measured for shoes, eat some bread and milk in John Macleod's house, shook hands with more than a dozen people, and was promised some shot by John McDonald. On the sand as I was returning I shot a gull and a sandpiper. Rory Bethune accompanied me on his way to the Cuddie fishing at Bun-an-Ois. A very fine day.

Wednesday.

Yesterday I was so lazily inclined that I did nothing more than skin a bird, and pick the fish out of some shells that I intended for preservation. So very lethargic was I that while reading the Pleasures of Hope upon the top of a hill near the house I actually fell asleep. Upon awaking, I in reality found myself under the impression that I had put off my mortal garments, and thought me entering upon some new scene. I could not help ejaculating a few words with great fervour, by way of prayer. In the afternoon Mr McLeod the St Kilda minister came to the house.

Today, before I got out of bed, a letter* was handed to me. What was my joy. O Craigie! (A student friend in Aberdeen) on discovering that the indorsation was in thy hand writing. Friend of my heart! said I, by the God of Heaven, I swear eternal fidelity to thee! On getting up I read it to my uncle and his wife who were yet in bed.

The weather yesterday was very fine. Today it is thick, rainy & blowy. But I find that in rainy weather I am sometimes more cheerful & light than in the finest. Perhaps I cannot account for it otherwise than upon the principles of contrast and variety. Yet these are scarcely sufficient. I enjoy good enough health, being only now and then troubled with a disagreeable sensation bordering upon pain in the left side of my thorax at its upper part. I am in much better condition, as graziers call it, than while at Aberdeen - and well I may, if cramming and exercise be sufficient for fattening one.

Thursday

Yesterday afternoon, while I was inoculating some children, Kenneth MacKenzie of Stornoway came in. He had travelled from Rodill to see me. To this latter place he had come in a vessel of his father's to Glasgow. The afternoon in course was

---

* With this letter MacGillivray also received two bacteriological plates. In the next entry in the journal he describes inoculating children, presumably against smallpox, with material from Aberdeen.

spent socially. About six Mrs Mac and I took a walk as far as Traigh-na-Clibhadh, and returned by the sands. After tea we fell a dancing with John McDiarmid for a musician. The commonality here take great delight in this exercise and are in general surprisingly expert at it. The minister, and Kenneth and I slept in the same apartment. We talked a little of bigotry and fanaticism, touching upon the character of the Gaelic schoolmaster who accompanied me last year from Marig to Tarbert, and some others similarly malined, in particular a man in Stornoway, who does not eat an egg that is laid on Sunday.

By the bye, none but ministers are dignified with the title of master here, at least among the nobility. Our parochial pastor for instance, is called Master Alexander, a neighbouring one Master Hugh. This, of whom I was lately speaking, Master Lachlan; though in that case the title is given merely through complaisance - as Lachlan is no regularly reared clergyman, but a sort of holy lecturer and catechist. He has left St Kilda for want of accomodations in a domiciliary way, and does not intend to return till these be furnished. His salary however appears to be regularly paid. He is a short robusteous fellow with a black coat and white wig, plays a little on the fiddle, violin I mean, not the Scotch fiddle, though perchance he may occasionally, i.e. by way of amusement take a scrape of it with a long bow, keeping time with his mouth, and prolonging & dulcifying the conclusory notes of each stave with a spirited exhalation or rather efflation through the nostrils, very much like the grunting of a hog. Master Lachlan takes snuff also, smokes tobacco, and he would leave not "the devil a drop" - albeit, nevertheless, furthermore, also, as Donald McKenzie says, he is not a bad fellow, though apparently a weak man. Kenneth further amused me with a story comprehending some of his exploits while in Glasgow. So without much ceremony we fell asleep, and for aught that I know to the contrary snored on till six o'clock. On rising we girded our loins with the top bands of our femoralia (breeches), shut the peep hole of the professor, and accoutred ourselves, just as we would have done, had we intended to stay out of bed all day - and this verily was our intention. So I accompanied Kenneth and the master as far as Carnan Mhic Thasgill, and wheeling about pursued my journey homewards spouting occasionally quotations from the Pleasures of Hope. So on returning I went to the milk house, as is my custom, and drank a dose of cow's milk. By the way, I may detail my stomachic economy - one might be worse employed. So - at eight or seven in the morning I drink warm milk, a chopin scots or so (a liquid measure of about half a pint), at ten take breakfast consisting of bread, potatoes, fish, butter, cheese and tea or milk, at four or five or six dependent upon circumstance, dine, i.e. eat soup, mutton, bundatoes, as Murdoch McLellan calls them, and turnips - at eight drink milk along with Miss Marion and the dairy maid who is blind of an eye, and at nine or ten either drink tea or milk with bread & butter or potatoes. Yesterday, while walking with Mary I counted twenty and one ravens seated near us - the day before I numbered ten ravens and three eagles flying along the brow of Bencapval.

Tuesday.

Since last report, the time has passed most agreeably, under the enjoyment of partly real and partly anticipated felicity. On Thursday Mr McNiel of St Kilda, his son Roderick of Kyles, and his grandson Wiliam called here on their way to Borve. William remained till his friends returned. After dining very heartily they set off. My uncle and I accompanied them as far as the temple, as it is called, of South town where we remained till sunset.

On Friday, after breakfast, I went to Borve taking two horses and a boy with one - my intention in so doing was to bring over Miss Christina Bethune and the Minister's children, who had promised last Sunday to spend a day with us. The weather proving very rainy I could not prevail upon her ladyship to accompany me, but obtained their consent to carry over the two boys, who were at Scarista at the school. William, however, proving sick, I was obliged to content me with Master Niel and scampered along the sand of Capval with a wet back.

On Saturday the weather was remarkably fine, a messenger had come from Rodill last night to tell me that the child I had been visiting had grown worse, so I was necessitated to go down today. I left North town about five o'clock, and returned about ten without the occurrence of any thing very worthy of notation. The child was in a dying state with squinting eyes and general spasms. I administered nothing - at twelve I set out for Borve with the boy and horses I had yesterday - at Scarista- I met the schoolmaster who was on his way to Kelligray - the boys had gone home. On arriving at Borve I shook hands with the members of the family, and desired the peregrinators to make ready. So we set out. Miss Christina Bethune, and her niece Isabella upon one horse, and William on the other, while Helen and I walked hand in hand. On crossing the sand, on which lay a good deal of water, Miss Christina rode alone. William and Isabella on the other horse. I carried Nelly in my arms till we were met by my uncle's cart - dined - walked in the evening to South town, where we sat for a long time & returned altogether. After tea the children, and Mrs McG and her sister Marion, and Miss Bethune danced some reels. I experienced great delight on seeing the children altogether on the floor. They constituting two of the most lovely couples that could well be seen, especially William and Isabella - The latter is I think the most beautiful little angel I have seen - I was quite bewitched with her eyes - what a charming portrait she would make! When tired of dancing we fell to amuse ourselves with little plays, such as Jack's alive, Blind Harry, and such. It was after twelve, i.e. Sunday morning before we got to bed.

On Sunday we got up about nine. I bathed at South town. After breakfast we formed a little party consisting of myself. Miss Marion, and the children, and ascended Ben Capval to the summit. Here we had a very fine view - I raised some of the stones which had fallen from Carn Uilliam. We descended by Carnach bhan, rolling fragments of rock down the declivity - which is very rapid. At South town we got wild carrots from some young people who were occupied in pulling them and gathered dulce (an edible seaweed) on Ru an teambuill. On returning we found that the rest had gone to Moll on a walk. They returned about four, and about six we dined. Then forth we sallied, steering for Ui - on the plains of which we scampered till the dusk, when we returned & drank tea. It was after twelve before we bedded.

Yesterday about twelve o'clock, we all set out for Scarista - Mrs MacGillivray on one horse, I and William Bethune on another, Miss Christina Bethune, my uncle, Niel, Isabella and Helen in the cart. I accompanied Miss Bethune to Borve - the children staid at the school. I promised to Mr Bethune to stay with them on Wednesday night and offered my services in explaining the principles of my beloved science Botany. At Scarista I drank some whisky with my uncle & John Macdonald merchant, and some others - My uncle & his wife seated themselves on one horse, and I on the other, without a saddle and carrying some small packets - and thus we rode till we were advanced some way upon the sand, when I lost a packet, and dismounting returned for it without leading my horse. The consequence was I could not overtake him, and was obliged to walk along, through the ford. Nothing more worth speaking that night, save, perchance, that I swallowed six cups of tea.

Today I rose about ten, after taking a dose of warm milk in bed - The weather was bad until near four in the evening - nothing done - about dusk I went with Marion to the fold.

Wednesday.

Rose about eight, went to Ui to search for a good specimen of the Common Scarlet Pimpernel. I found some in a field of barley, and returned. In drawing this flower I was occupied till half past two. Two of my old scholars Roderick Bethune and Roderick Maclennan came over from Scarista with a pound of gun powder and six of shot from John Mcdonald. This being the day on which I promised to go to Borve, I set out after dinner. On the sand near North town I shot two Sanderlings and proceeded accompanied by the two boys mentioned toward the sea in expectation of finding shells upon its shore. Our walk was very fatiguing, owing to the softness of the sand caused by its having lately been covered by rain water. Nearly opposite to Scarista we fell in with a herd of women busily employed in catching sand-eels, and were mightily amused with seeing a race between a dozen of them having their petticoats kilted above the knee. The women in this country are very robusteous, and their legs are not in common behind in the proportion. I pitied much a poor old woman, scarcely able to stand whom I saw picking up a few on the dry part of the sand. Small flocks of Sanderlings occurred occasionally. This species is almost always to be found on the sand of North town as well as the Ringed Plover. The latter seldom appears in flocks. At Ceann na Sgeiradh, I observed that the sand had concressed into a stony substance lying in plates upon the surface. It appears however to lie naturally under the drifting or loose sand, and to be mixed with clay or some similar substance, for it is much darker than the other. We had found some shells upon the sand. Rory Bethune carried them and the birds to Scarista, while I accompanied by Maclennan proceeded. I was very kindly received by the family at Borve. They had just dined as I arrived. Mr Bethune and I talked upon various subjects till night fell, when we drank tea. After tea Mr B. began to read the Systema Natura of Linnous (Linnaeus), which together with Smith's Compendium I had brought over for his inspection: while we i.e. Miss Chra. Bethune, myself, Niel, William, Isabella & Helen amused ourselves with little tricks of a nature similar to those we had recourse to at North town. Says one to his neighbour, "Cupid is come," "How is he come?" asks the other. He is come anxious, and so on, giving each letter of the alphabet a round. In the same manner Aaron's beard was described, for example says one Aaron's beard was an awful beard, Aaron's beard says the next was an alarming beard, an arable beard adds a third - 2nd round - Aaron's beard was a bouncing beard, a boisterous beard, a bristly beard. Put this about says one. What's that? asks his neighbour - my lady's lap dog, and so round - at each gradation a new sentence was a song till the whole came to be. Ten station dancing masters teaching a parrot to speak, nine (nothing written here. He obviously couldn't remember what nine was), eight elephants dancing a minuet, seven separate solicitations from seven separate counties, six (forgotten as well), five flip flap flat bottomed fly boats, four blind cats eating grishkin, three camels cropping cauliflower, two cherry trees, and my lady's lap dog. About eleven I retired to bed, and slept very soundly in a very comfortable bed till about six.

Thursday.

Rose today about six, and sallied forth with my gun accompanied by Niel and William. The morning was rather dullish, but the weather promised to be good. At little Borve I shot a pigeon, saw the Mare's Tail and Long-leaved Water Speedwell, & visited a sick child of Kenneth Macleod's. Before we had returned, the schoolmaster and the two young ladies had set out for Scarista. I regretted much that I had not been in time to see Miss Isabel. Her face is so beautiful that one might gaze for ever at it. On returning I examined the Water Speedwell, and the Pig and Goose from domesticated individuals. After breakfast I went to Loch na Cartach, a rushy lake about a mile from Borve, in hopes of finding ducks. I did not succeed in killing any, though I fired several shots. On the way back I gathered flowers, and on regaining the house found my uncle seated in the parlour. We set off for Luskentir with a horse between us. We arrived about four and dined. In the evening the gentry took a walk, while I sneaked into a burial ground near the house, and sat me down upon a grave, that appeared to have been newly tennanted. Here I indulged in some serious reflection, and decyphered an Alas! upon a stone at the head of the grave. The evening was passed in conversation, which I could not relish - We retired at a late hour.

Friday

Rose about nine - breakfasted - went to a small lake near the house in search of ducks, but found none. Mr Stewart had to go to the hills to see some sheep - we agreed to accompany him. Our crew consisted of Mr Stewart, Mr McKinlay, my uncle, myself, and three country lads. The wind blew pretty fresh, and the sea was not very smooth, so the rowers were something tired before we reached our destination

Loch Leosabhidh. By the way, we passed through the Kyle between the two islands of Soay. From the sea, here, one has a very good view of highland scenery. This part of the country is very rugged and bleak - Some deer are found in the hills - we were disappointed in seeing the sheep there being none there. So we shoved off with three barrels of tar on board - We sailed part and rowed part of the way. I fired at a Solan goose (Gannet) on the wing, & took it down, but it managed to get away. In coming out of the boat, my uncle slipped, and fell plump into the sea, drawing Mr McKinlay along with him. Mr Stewart however laid hold of the latter, and we succeeded in dragging both ashore. It was five before we regained the house. After tea, the company which consisted of - Donald Stewart Esq, the landlord, Alexander and Archibald his brothers, Mrs Stewart, Mr McKinlay, surgeon, & country physician, Kenneth Macleod from Tarnsay - Mr McFarlane, teacher to Stewart's children, and my uncle fell a talking about some stuff of their own, while I sick of the place fled to Nature for relief. It was near nine o'clock. The sky was cloudy - excepting in the east - the moon was rising over Buillibhal - and the north and east were illuminated with the Aurora Borealis. It was particularly brilliant in the north - but I could only see an occasional glimpse of it between the thick clouds which every where formed a broad curtain along the verge of the horizon. A semiarch of pale white ran along from the east in a waving manner. I was delighted with the scene. On a hill before the house, where I enjoyed this spectacle I planned a poem to be begun soon, and after spouting pieces of the Pleasures of Hope returned. I spoke some to Mr McFarlane, who as I have said turned out to be one of those who had treated me so kindly last summer - when benighted on Benvenue. I had apologised yesterday for not recognizing him at Borve, though in fact I had little occasion. He is a very good looking young man. After drinking some toddy we bedded about twelve o'clock.

Saturday.

Got up a little after five, and after spending some time in making preparation for our journey set out. The Redshank is common along the ford of Luskentir. On the sand, besides the Mallard, we saw the Common Gull and Oystercatcher; the latter in abundance. While my uncle trudged slowly along on horseback I went round the Marsh of Nisbost in expectation of getting some coots, but I did not succeed. At Borve we fell in with the schoolmaster and the boys who accompanied us as far as Scarista. So we got home before nine, and breakfasted heartily. Till dinner time I occupied myself in writing some of these notes, and in trifling away my time between Marion and my gun. In the evening I went to the fold with Marion. After supper Mary played at Backgammon with me. So to shorten a long story, I retired to my bed chamber, and went to bed when I found it convenient. Before this came to pass however I had laid the following plan for regulating my conduct during the ensuing week -

Sleep from five to eight hours in twenty four proportioned to the degree of exhaustion. Each day I must walk at least five miles - Give at least half a dozen puts to a heavy stone, make six leaps! Drink milk twice a day, wash my face, ears, teeth and feet, and rise with or before the sun. Seven specimens of natural history must be preserved, whether in propria persona or by drawing. I must study to live well, i.e. virtuously - to be particular I must abstain from cursing and swearing - must endeavour to be always cheerful & anxious to please, must pay the strictest regard to my honour, especially in the article of promises. Each night after the labours of the day are over I shall note any remarkable incidents that may have occurred through the day, & take a review of my conduct. In the morning I shall sketch a plan for the day. Above all procrastination is to be shunned - every opportunity seized with eagerness and in short a complete change is to take place in my conduct, and such a change as is pointed out by season, and is likely to be approved of at the end of the week. Some of these articles cannot apply to Sunday.

Sunday.

Rose early, took a towel in my pocket, and went over to South town where I washed in the sea. The water felt very cold. Here I observed a flock of ducks, and an immense squadron of scarts passing from their habitacles at the west side of Bencapval to their fishing stations up the sound. The gannet too was fishing. On my way home, I fell in with the cattle, and drank some warm milk - after breakfast I went over to South town in quest of flowers. On returning I prepared for a journey to Scarista, where we were informed there was to be a preaching. Miss Marion accompanied me. Mr Macleod of Marig preached - the sermon was very indifferent - Miss Bethune from Borve and the children, and Duncan McLellan of Ensay, and William McKenzie from Tarbert were all the people of note that I saw. The money collected amounted to thirteen pence halfpenny. Mr Macleod accompanied us to North town. The day was uncommonly fine. After dinner, the ladies and I took a walk to South town, not as people walk in towns but after our own warm highland manner - with my left hand upon Mary's right shoulder, and my right arm about Marion's waist - Our conversation was light and desultory. Miss Marion and I then went to the fold. She has a very good figure and face, but is rather deficient in point of education. She is in short a stout, hale, buxom, highland wench. When we were at tea a gentleman from Uist, Mr Dingwal, came in. I retired soon after, and taking a great coat of Mary's about my shoulders walked solitarily over to the hill of Tashtir. It was about nine of a very fine night - I stood upon an eminence. There was a gentle breeze from the north, the moon shone in a clear skye, thinly sprinkled with stars - the broad line of reflection commencing at the island of Ensay and terminating at Traigh-na-clibhadh showed by the degrees of brightness the different currents in the channel. To the north west the great ocean opened - to the south the sound of Skye. Between these lay, at the distance of some miles the islands Ensay, Berneray and Pabbay, while the hills of Hirta veyed the horizon - The gentle rustling of the corn waving in the breeze, the ripple of the wavelet on the shore, and the scream of the wandering sea bird gave life to the scene. On the other side I had the hills of Harris, those in the distance tipped with gray mist. I recited some pieces of poetry, returned home, and after writing these notes retired to bed about twelve o'clock.

Saturday.

On Monday last I rose about day break, and sallied forth with my gun and Mr Macleod's dog Bounce. One snipe was all that I shot. After breakfast Messrs. Dingwal and McLeod departed - the former to go home, the latter to proceed to Borve, where I was to meet him tonight. Bounce attended me to the hills, on the opposite side of the strand. I met the Gaelic schoolmaster of Strond, who told me he was much troubled with headach, and requested my advice. I found that his complaint was hypochondriosis, and advised him to use a purgative occasionally, and to drink a decoction of chamomile or centaury every morning. After traversing the moor between Inis-shi and Borve by a circuitous rout I arrived at the latter place about four o'clock. I had only shot one plover by the way. After dinner we conversed on various subjects, particularly poetry and Natural History. In the evening Aaron's beard was again described, and some other little tricks performed, in all which Mr McLeod assisted with great good humour.

On Tuesday I was up by sunrise. I searched the Minister's wintering ground for grouse, but found none. I shot however two plovers and returned to breakfast. On my way to the moor again Mr McLeod accompanied me as far as the old fortification. No game, excepting one snipe which I shot, occurred till I reached Druim nan Caorach where I shot a moorfowl. The weather this day as well as on Monday and Sunday proved remarkably fine. Emerging from the mountains by the pass at Inis-shi I crossed the sand to North town, walking for a great part of the way with my eyes shut. As I had recrossed the sands, I was met by a girl whom I had seen last year at North town, Oibhrig nighean Ioin ghairbh - she accompanied me as far as Borve carrying my bundle - At Scarista I got some snuff from John Macdonald, and fell in with Niel Bethune. In the evening we played at Blind Harry. Mhaighstir Paterson &c. at the former I gave myself such a furious blow against the wall that I fell on the floor half senseless. Mr Macleod with great glee contributed his share to the sport. I had read part of my journal to him and the ladies before tea, and now was obliged in paying one of my forfeits to recite a piece of poetry of my own composition. We slept soundly till nine o'clock next day. Mr Macleod and I strolled into the garden, where I eat some pease. About one o'clock we set out for Nisbost, where we passed the night agreeably with Mr Torrie. Here I saw Mr and Mrs MacNabb - Mr Stewart called on his way to Rodill, and invited us to go there tomorrow night for the purpose of celebrating the Laird's marriage. On Thursday the weather proving very wet and boisterous the gentlemen did not accompany me to Rodill. Mr Macleod however came over to Borve. At Borve I saw Mr and Mrs Bethune and drank a glass of whisky. At Scarista went to the schoolhouse for the sole purpose of seeing Miss Isabella. Beyond little Scarista I overtook Mr Donald Campbell of Tarnsay on his way to Rodill, but was obliged to leave him to go to North town. At North town I shaved and got a horse. It was about five o'clock when I reached Rodill. Dinner was over. After shifting in John Macdonald's I accompanied the gentlemen to the park near Macleod's house. Here a bonfire consisting of a considerable quantity of peats was burning. The rain had ceased, and the wind blew very freshly from the South. I had been wetted to the skin in coming, but soon dried at the bonfire. On the eminences on which the fire blazed stood Donald Stewart the Factor, my uncle, Mr MacKinlay, Mr Donald Campbell, Donald and John Macdonald Merchants, John Macdonald alias Sir John Stobbie, and Duncan MacLellan of Ensay; while a little below the Tennantry were ranged in order. The health of the gentlemen present was first drunk!! Next that of the Laird - then that of the lady. The nobility then danced a few reels on

46

the green to the bagpipe. The boys were merry. The whole party in the dusk of the evening marched, preceeded by the piper to the Laird's house in each of the front windows of which excepting one a solitary candle was burning. A few reels were danced before the door, and some very irregular hurraing kept up. Some of the men were said to be tipsey. The boys were in excellent glee. There was no fighting however. On returning to the public house, we drank tea, and soon after commenced bouzing. The company consisted of those mentioned, and Mr Dingwal of Uist, and Malcolm Macdonald of Rodill. So we drank on till near twelve, when a piper was called and a few women procured, and we fell a capering very nimbly on the floor. Och! by the powers! we were in good trim for it - Donald Campbell danced with me. In spite of all I could do, the piper would not give us long reels. I do not know that I ever felt so very keen for dancing. About half past two the dancing stopped, and drinking began again, and was continued till four when we bedded. On Friday we got up about nine, and breakfasted about eleven. At one I set out, mounted on my gray horse. I rode in the common way till I passed the Mill. But here the story of the Count Schaumberg coming to mind, I determined to turn my face to the horse's tail, and thus to ride on till I should be obliged to desist. As the bridle I had was of no use in this way of riding I tied it about the horse's neck, and proceded at an easy trot - nor did I stop till I found myself before the house at Northtown. In the evening my uncle and Donald Campbell arrived. After tea two tar barrels were set on fire near the house, and the healths of Macleod and his lady drank by us and my uncle's servants and one or two others. Some reels were also danced with great spirit - and in the house the capering was kept up till three in the morning - After which we drank a tumbler of toddy and bedded.

Today I got up about ten - Nothing worthy of notice occurred today. I was in a sulky mood for a great part of the day. A day of apathy - The pain in my breast has recurred tonight. In regard to my resolutions of last Saturday, I have only to say that none of them has been regarded. A new week however begins tomorrow, and I shall see how well I shall behave.

Wednesday, October, 1817.

Since last report the time has passed most agreeably. I have traversed considerable tracts of ground, have confirmed old friends & made new. Last Sunday the weather was bad. Showers of sleet with a keen northerly wind. I crossed the sand and ascended the hill of Maodal. From the summit I enjoyed a very fine spectacle. Beneath my feet lay the farm of Drimafuinnd the plains of Ui, and the far extending sand of Capval. Before me the hill of North town, the ocean covered with showering clouds, showing in their interstices glimpses of sunshine, and at times the islands of St Kilda - on the right hand the summits of the hills terminated by Clisham, and the long ridge which extends from it to the island of Scarp. On the left the channel with its rocks & islands bounded by the low sands of Uist. I observed that the showers in their fall formed a line inclining in a direction contrary to the wind. On the ridge between Maodal and Ronaval I saw a Snow-bunting, and on the latter hill gathered some mineralogical specimens. In returning along the shore by the low hills of Drimafuinnd I saw another Snow-bunting.

On Monday I left North town about ten o'clock with the intention of going to Borve to meet Mr Macleod the minister with whom I was to proceed by Scalpay to Marig and then to Valamis in Lewis, where the asbestus is found. On arriving at Scarista I learned that Mr McLeod had not yet passed to Borve. So I remained there till evening, when I accompanied the schoolmaster to Borve. Mr McLeod arrived late - the evening passed merrily.

On Tuesday we got up early - left Borve, and breakfasted with Mr Torrie at Nisbost - we then proceeded by the sand and hill of Luskentir to Ceann Dibig. Near this bay I saw a species of duck new to me upon one of the lakes and several specimens of Red Grouse occurred. Here the parson baptized a female child. I had the honour of being made Gosti. We partook of some refreshment which the poor people offered us. It consisted of potatoes, herring and excellent cream. I seldom dined more contentedly. The subject of meat introduced a little story which I may relate. One day as the late Fear of Luskentir, Doctor Macleod, was passing one of his bays, he entered the house of a poor tenant. It was in the harvest season. The good woman of the house pressed him to wait until she should prepare some refreshment for him - and he to gratify her wishes assented. So a sheaf of oats was brought in from the field, the ears burnt off, winnowed and ground in less than twenty minutes. The meal was next sifted, baked and toasted: and a cake of oatbread placed before him, on which and a proportionate quantity of good cream he made a hearty repast. I mention this to show with what celerity bread may be prepared by people possessed of a hand mill or quern. The whole process was performed in the space of a half hour, and in this time the corn which stood in the field was placed in the form of bread upon the table. In such a country as this where the land is rocky, & mountainous, intersected with lakes and lochs, the hand mill becomes a very useful, and almost indispensable instrument - at least to the poor farmer. The good man Aonas MacDhomhnuill 'ic (son of) Ioin bhan, with another poor tennant ferried us over to another bay, at the distance of two or three miles Urga. I had previously inoculated three of his children gratis. The minister would not go to Scalpay. So we put up at the house of a very decent man, where we were most hospitably entertained. They have a notion in this country of tea being the most acceptable to genteel strangers of all potable substances. It was in consequence prepared for us, but I relished more the simple and indigenous fare of Ceann-dibig. To supper we had tea, bread, butter, cheese and fish - the fish was the yearling of the coal fish, which is plentiful over the whole country. The good man told us the greatest number he ever killed at once was nine score and odds. From one to five scores is the usual number, and this is great when we consider that not more than two hours at most are spent in the employment. The weather had been cold and snowy, and apprehensions began to be entertained of a bad harvest.

On Wednesday we rose about nine, and breakfasted. About ten we made our departure. The reason of our lying so long today, was that over night we had been so harassed by the attack of irregular troops of light armed cavalry, as to be prevented from sleeping. Near Urga a very pretty piece of highland scenery occurred. It consisted of a dark lake, a rocky hill, with goats on the verge of a precipice intent on us who were passing below. The hail came in great showers, the wind was exceedingly keen, and the summits of the hills were covered with snow. I left the parson a little above Marig, and proceeded toward Clisheim. In despite of hail and snow, and frost and whirlwinds I clambered to the summit, and well was my labour repaid: for from this I enjoyed a very sublime spectacle. I was on the highest pinnacle of that range of islands denominated the Long Island, throned upon a precipitous ridge of rocks. The islands of Uist, Harris and Lewis lay under my feet. Toward the east & south in the extreme distance appeared the mountains of Ross and Inverness shires, with the hills and capes and plains of Skye. Toward the west a long series of pointed summits, commencing at Clisheim, forming a broad ridge, intersected transversely by broad vallies, extended for several miles. They appeared to be much lower than the hill on which I stood, and resembled heaps of sand formed by pouring it from a vessel. The snow lay pretty deep upon them all - and the whirlwinds sweeping along their ridges appeared most beautifully sublime. I was enveloped in one, but it did not happen to prove very boisterous. The great ocean was covered with clouds. I viewed the subjacent country of Lewis, flat & covered with lakes, and with considerable difficulty descended into a deep valley to the north east of Clisheim. When I was here, the snow came on so thickly, that I was apprehensive of being smothered in it. I felt too for the first time perhaps the disagreeable effects of cold - my feet and fingers were almost senseless, and I began to feel sickish and faint. I got warm however by walking briskly, and after passing the deep glen of Langadal sat me down upon the western side of it to take a pinch of snuff. It was my intention to go to Luachar, to see some old friends and I was now in a part of the country utterly unknown. At parting with the minister, I had got directions, to be sure, but he talked so heterogeneously of hills and passes and glens and rivers and lakes, that I learned just as much from him as if he had said nothing at all. I heard him however with patience. In order to make me quite sure of the road, he sketched a plan for me, an exact copy of which is annexed (not in this journal) - I could scarcely keep my gravity, yet I took it thankfully and proceeded - Now after taking a pinch, I ascended an eminence forming a pass between two mountains near the head of Loch Languad a lake upwards of twelve miles in length, though my friend had marked it in his plan as a small oval pond. From this I discovered marks of cultivation at the distance of three of four miles, and accordingly steered toward the spot, walking along a stream that ran in this direction. By this stream I saw a herd of deer consisting of seven, and observed some bothies built entirely of stone which Mr Macleod, I now recollected had told me of. So by this mark I thought me sure of being in the right course. Accordingly in the dusk the house appeared, and I entered without being perceived. Ewen MacDiarmid and his wife Christina McAskill were sitting at the fire. "Are you busy?" asked I familiarly. Christy rose & took me by the hand. Ewen did not recognize me at first, but he quickly came to his senses. So I got seated by a furious peat fire - a servant took off my pedicles, washed my feet, then dried them, & covered them with a clean pair of stockings. Supper followed in course!

On Thursday I got out of bed about ten - we breakfasted about eleven, and about twelve went up by the stream, the course of which I had followed yesterday, in expectation of falling in with deer I had seen. As we were passing the side of a hill about a mile and a half from the house, Ewen observed two stags above us. We proceeded without stopping - and when a few hundred yards farther on I slipped behind a hillock, while he went to the opposite hill and sat down in order to attract the attention of the animals. In a few minutes I had got within twelve yards, and was proceeding to take the beasts up, as it is called, when I heard "Come away," "Come away" from the valley below. I hesitated for some time to arise, but another couple of come-aways determined me. I lifted my head, when the deer started up and scampered away. I fired at one, but did not kill it. Ewen had thought that the animals had gone away, and was afraid that I would occupy too much time, in crawling about the place where they had been. He proceeded up the glen, crossed a hill, observed a small herd upon a mountain, steered homeward, saw two beyond reach, & arrived before dark.

On Friday we traversed the hills and glens to the west of Luachar. The scenery was as romantic as it could be without wood. An immense rock at the entrance of a glen or pass between the mountains, in particular, attracted my attention. In this glen is a cave, capable, it is said of containing a hundred men, which had been the place of retreat of a gentleman of the country, after the unfortunate battle of Culloden, and under the great rock is a spot impregnably fortified by the hand of nature, which had been held in days of yore by a famous free-booter. The cave derives its name as well as the glen from a satyr who formerly resided there. So says tradition - and so believes superstition. I was told by my friendly guide that Ulladil, the Urisk or satyr, one day followed a man who was said to be the strongest in the Long Island as far as Luachar. The man seeing he could not escape, put his back to a stone to be seen there to this day, determined to sell his life as dearly as possible. They grappled and tore each other till both fell. The dying man desired his servant, who had accompanied him but who it seems stood aloof during the combat, to bury them one on each side of the stone - and here they still remain. It might be worth while to dig up the place, as a careful search would either prove or disprove the authenticity of the fact. In the evening as we were descending a lofty hill, Ewen discovered some deer on a gentle declivity below us. We counted to the number of eleven. After some crawling and running, I contrived to get within shot, and getting an opportunity at one fired. The ball had missed, but the swan shot took effect. The animal lingered behind the rest who scampered quickly away unable to ascend the hill after them. Night fell, and we were in course obliged to leave off the pursuit. It was late before we reached Luachar, as we travelled four miles over a very rugged and soft tract.

On Saturday I left Ewen near the house, and had not gone far before I observed a small herd consisting of five. Of these I managed to kill one. After this I proceeded to a mountain glen, about a mile off when I found another herd of seven. I fired at a stag of them, but being at too great a distance did no execution. On returning to the place where the deer lay I met Ewen who was returning from searching for the one I had shot last night. He had proved successful, and had some of its viscera upon his back. So we cut open the other, and packed up some of it with the rest. Night had fallen before we arrived. Tonight we feasted upon venison. My food since my arrival here has been potatoes, salmon, mutton, milk, cream, and curds.

N.B. As this Report is misdated I must correct it by observing that the Sunday with which it commences was the 28th of September, and so on regularly, and without intermission to Saturday the 4th October with which it terminates.

North Town, Tuesday, 14th October, 1817.

On Sunday, the 5th, I left Luachar about mid day. As the deer lay near the way I intended to take, I proposed to decapitate them, & carry the spoils on my back to North town, and this I did. Ewen accompanied me as far as Strom nan Scurt, a prodigious rock in the pass of Miavag. Between this and Tarbert, the road, or rather rout, for there is scarcely any appearance of a foot path, lay over hills and heaths, rivers and bogs. The Common Ling is the predominant plant in these regions. The sun had set before I reached Tarbert, and night fell long before I attained the summit of Benluskentir. In course I made but slow progress upon the hill; and it was after twelve when I found myself seated upon a chair in my bedroom at North town.

On the evening of Monday the 6th word came from Rodell that Miss Jessy Macdonald of Ord, a cousin of Mrs McGillivray's, had arrived from Skye, my uncle in consequence went to meet her. I should have gone, had not my late journey put me completely out of trim. Mr Finlay MacRae came to the house in the dusk. The evening was spent agreeably. We conversed upon poetry and religion, and drank a little Rum punch.

On Tuesday, the 7th, my uncle arrived in the morning with Miss MacDonald, and Mr Finlay departed. After breakfast, I accompanied my uncle to Ard Nisbost, where there was to be an exhibition of stallions. Here I saw Messrs Stewart, Torrie, McKinlay, D. McLellan, Archd. Stewart & McLean the schoolmaster. Stewart gave me leave to shoot a deer. My uncle, the Doctor, and I are to form a party, on our way we called at Borve.

On Thursday, the 9th I was sent for by Duncan MacLellan of Ensay to visit a sick servant of his. As my uncle was anxious that I should go, I gave my assent. On the way I met my aunt Marcilla, with two of her children, from Glasgow. On arriving at Ensay I found a robust woman in her bed, senseless, motionless, speechless - pulse regular, slow and weak, breathing apparently easy. She had been but lately delivered of her first child, had gone out the evening before, taken milk at the fold, returned, sickened and complained of intense pain in her head. She had not spoken since ten o'clock of the preceding night, a lancet was thrust into her arm and about eight ounces of blood obtained. Shortly after she revived, spoke quite sensibly, recognized her friends, said she felt easy, excepting that she had a slight pain in her forehead. By the bye, a little gruel and whisky with caraway seeds had been given immediately after the bleeding. About nine at night she became delirious, and ten or twelve ounces of blood were taken. This again restored her to her senses. I lodged with Duncan - we played at cards. On the morning of Friday I got over to Kyles in Archibald Campbell's boat, and reached North town about nine o'clock.

On Saturday, the 11th my uncle and I sailed through the islands of Ensay on our way to Berneray. He shot a sea bird, and we landed on a sand bank where I obtained specimens of shell fish. In the evening we reached Kyles of Uist. The family here consists of Mr & Mrs McNiel, Masters William & Ewen and Miss Mary - The good man is a polite, well-formed, agreeable man, about fifty - He is suspected however of dishonesty, and does not bear a good character in regard to equity and humanity. Mrs McNiel is of the same age, has a curious phiz, (face) semicircular in profile, a rough voice, and not very agreeable manner - though she is said to have been handsome. This I deny: for her face, and person are quite at variance with the laws of proportion. Miss Mary is a pale faced, wry-necked, ackward girl - poor creature! She looked like one dying of love, or troubled with amenorrhoea. As to William & Ewen, the latter is a boy, the former a gigantic raw-boned, rough, illiterate, impolite - yet good hearted: and possibly honest fellow.

On Sunday, some business brought my uncle to the preaching - at about three miles distance from Kyles. Mr MacNiel and I accompanied him. Mr MacRae preached. The meeting house was thatched: yet having some good seats, and being well filled with a very decent and well-dressed congregation, appeared far superior to our parish church in Harris. After sermon Mr MacRae treated us with a mutchkin of aqua-vita. We returned in the evening. Mr MacNiel and my uncle retired to a tippling house at Kyles, while I walked into the parlour or dining-room, for it is both. Here I found Mary, and spoke a little to her.

Instead of tea, we drank in this house a liquor, which my uncle took for coffee, but the chief ingredient of which I discovered to be barley. It is very agreeable, and perhaps preferable to either tea or coffee. It is manufactured in this way: a cake of barley is baked, and toasted brown - it is then ground in a hand-mill & boiled in water, milk and sugar are added to complete the beverage. In the evening Kyles read a sermon of Blair's to us. I never felt a greater inclination to sleep, but I bore out, and enjoyed some very slight degree of pleasure in seeing William and Mary and latterly Mrs MacNiel fall asleep. In fact I never heard such an opified discourse. It was read with a low voice, a ridiculously affected delivery, and distorted pronounciation - Many words were mistaken - indeed I venture to assert that he did not understand what he read - after tea, or barley water, we drank some gin toddy, and about one retired to bed.

On Monday, the 13th, we rose about seven, breakfasted and left Kyles about nine. On our way to North town we landed at Ensay, where we saw Duncan and his wife. The sick woman whom I visited last week was keeping well - I had directed her to take no other food for some days than gruel and a little milk. She had been much troubled for some years before with violent headaches - of which she got rid by losing blood. The tide had turned against us - so after reaching the mainland side, we were obliged to row all the way to South town.

Miss McDonald is a very agreeable young lady. She is small and delicate, but enjoys good health. Her features are not regular but her complexion is fine, perhaps rather pallid. Her air is unassuming, her gait graceful - her manner attaching, her conversation lively and sensible. In short she is a very accomplished young lady: & though not a beauty, is yet agreeable - She and Mary and I have walked to the fold together these two nights.

Ever since the day, on which I ascended Clisheim the wind has continued from the north. The weather has in consequence been remarkably fine. Southerly and westerly winds bring rain - the latter storms. Northerly and easterly winds bring fine weather - the latter very dry, and is principally experienced in March and April. Westerly winds are the most frequent, and the climate is rainy and cold for the greater part of the year. This season, the weather has been upon the whole good, the crop is in consequence nearly secured in some places and in all is in a fair way.

Luachar, Saturday, 18th October.

I arrived here last night in quality of harbinger to a shooting party to be composed of my uncle, Doctor McKinlay, Mrs McGillivray, and Miss MacDonald. On the evening of Wednesday I took a long walk with Miss MacDonald and Miss Marion. The time passed most agreeably - The sun had set - the moon shone faintly. The bright purple, and crimson of the west were contrasted with the pale blue & dark clouds that covered the verge of the horizon in the north and east. The sea was smooth as a lake - the wind still & the air had a most exhilarating keenness. Next morning I occupied myself in preparing for an expedition to the hills - and about two o'clock left North town. At Scarista I visited a sick woman, and got some ammunition and snuff and tobacco from John MacDonald the Merchant, and an ink bottle from John Car. At Borve I dined with the family there - at Nisbost just spoke to Mr Torrie. Night had come on before I reached Luskentir. Here I found Mr Stewart, Mr McKinlay and Mr McFarlane, the two former had just returned from an unsuccessful expedition to the hills in search of a place fit for planting. After taking tea we drank each two tumblers of whisky punch and bedded. Yesterday breakfasted about nine, and about ten departed. I ascended the hill nearer the house than usual - and on the summit, and along the northern side gathered several mineralogical specimens. After leaving Tarbert I struck through a mountain glen near Clisheim, called Bealach an Scail, and crossing a steep hill entered another glen, which led to a third stretching toward the extremity of Loch Rezort, the western boundary of Harris, at which I arrived a little after night had fallen. Here I got my stockings changed and dined. The evening passed agreeably, in conversation, making a snuff box, snuffing, supping and smoking. Mrs McDiarmid has got a young son - One of her sisters was in attendance upon her - she is "a sweet sonsy lass" as Robie says.

Today, after breakfast, I set out to the hills with my gun, alone. The weather was delightfully serene. I returned in the dusk without having got any sport, although I travelled a great deal and saw some deer. The wild animals I saw yesterday between Tarbert and Luachar were the Raven, Hooded Crow, Meadow Pipit, a small gray hawk unknown to me, the Common Gull and Heron. In the upper end of Gleann Staoladil I heard a stag bellowing - and near Luachar, I heard the snipe also.

At the close of a week, I generally repent of my sins, and form resolutions - which are never fulfilled. I shall not now however sketch a plan for the regulation of my conduct during the ensuing week - but merely promise to behave upon the whole romantically! I shall be more minute than usual in my details, and shall not fail to note my remarks, observations, and narrative, with the greatest regularity, & in the best order I can devise.

Preparatively to this, let me describe the scenery, shooting ground, house and its inhabitants. The scenery is generally of the grand order with little or no beauty. We have a long series of lofty mountains, running into ridges, & forming deep glens. These mountains are all rugged & precipitous, they run north-east and south-west. Stretching toward the north from them are low hills and extensive plains several miles in length and toward the south higher hills & vallies. On the declivities and under the rocks are the haunts of the deer, not easily found by a stranger, but well known to the inhabitants. Loch Rezort terminates the ground of sport on the north, the ocean on the west and south, and the Lewes on the east. The whole ground is broken into little eminences & depressions, covered with heath and some other plants - at this season of the year of a yellowish, or brown colour, which renders it extremely difficult to see the deer - though the broken nature of the surface facilitiates an approach to them when discovered. The house, our place of rendezvous, is situated at the distance of between one and four miles from the places of resort of the deer, at the head of an arm of the sea which constitutes part of the northern boundary of Harris. It is what in the Hebrides is denominated a black house and what Dr Johnson calls a hut. Its inhabitants are Ewen McDiarmid, a shepherd in the employment of a gentleman of Kintail who has a very extensive tract in Harris under sheep, a rough, unpolished, but honest and civil man advanced in years; his wife Christina McCaskill, daughter of Mr McCaskill schoolmaster of Uig in Lewis, a genteel woman of about thirty; little John their son, a comical cross grained boy; two female servants, the one a clumsy lump, the other a half-idiot with only one eye.

Luachar, Thursday, 30th October.

On Sunday, the 19th, Ewen and Miss Nelly and I and little John went to Toray, a small farm two miles down Loch Rezort on the Lewis side. One of our incitements to go there was to see two children of Ewen's who were lodged there. Here we were treated with cream and potatoes. I made a very hearty repast. The vessels which held the cream were only two in number, so the good-man and the good-woman and Ewen were placed about one, while Miss Nelly and I got the other. Had any other arrangement been made, I had been disgusted, and I could not refuse to partake of their fare, without being liable to the imputation of pride. We returned in the evening.

On Monday, 20th, the weather was unfavourable for shooting, being very rainy. So I contented myself with fishing upon a lake about two miles from the house. I caught about twenty trouts. In the evening as I was sitting by the fire, half naked, and drying myself, who should come in but my uncle, Mr McG, Miss McDonald and their attendants. The Doctor had not joined the party.

On Tuesday and Wednesday we traversed the hills without success. A man from Kinrezort accompanied my uncle as guide, while I scampered along alone. They fired several shots, while I did not see a single deer. In one of my expeditions I entered the cave of Ulladil, accompanied by a servant, several plants grew in it e.g. the Common Wood-sorrel, Common Chickweed, a fern, and a moss unknown. We drank with my shoe, a draught or two of water from the well, but soon relented for it left us sickish for a considerable time.

Thursday was spent in the same way - nothing was shot by either party - Mr McCaskill came over to see his daughter & niece.

On Friday, the 24th, we all left Luachar, with the intention of going to Uig. About two miles from the house, we observed a small herd of deer, consisting of five. Little worthy of remark occurred till we reached Timisgarry in Uig - on the west side of the Lewes, and about twelve miles from Luachar. The day had been tolerably good, but the road was very rugged - Hills and glens and lakes compose the whole scenery - not a blade of soft or meadow grass was seen in the whole route. After dining in Mr MacCaskill's we were visited by two ladies of the minister's family who invited me to drink tea with them. This invitation was of course accepted. Mr Hugh Munro is an old man of clear complexion, sub-sickly, sub grave phiz, not very robust habit. He wears a white cotton nightcap - aye - even in the pulpit. His two daughters are accomplished girls. Katherine is on the list of old maids is said to have been beautiful. I deny this - Her lips are thin as paper. It is verily queer that the Hebrideans should esteem thin lips and linear eyebrows as beautiful. As to my own opinion on the subject - Oh! by the powers! rosy cheeks and pouting lips. Marion has a genteel figure, an excellent face, with a nose of taste, and a mouth of eloquence!

On Sunday we went to church. The kirk is a thatched house, without regular seats, and having a most miserable pulpit composed of a few fir sticks. I did not see a good female face in the congregation. Mr Munro, honest man, is but a lame preacher - in good sooth I thought he was but a man of mean parts when I first saw him.

Dined and drank tea in his house. Master Alexander Simson, who had come here last evening, conducted himself with great politeness, while I, poor booby! sat sulky in a corner - and why? because I could not relish the conversation. It consisted of scandal - A minister's house, Sunday evening, a professed Christian & servant of God, light conversation, scandal, strangers - these cannot be reconciled.

Monday proved boisterous - and we kept the house all day. In the evening I drew two flounce patterns for the Munroes.

On Tuesday, the 18th left Uig - After travelling upwards of a mile we took a boat, and rowed up to near the head of Loch Rog, where we entered a shepherd's house. Mrs MacNaughton, the good-wife treated us with warm milk, potatoes and cheese. She is a most excessively kind woman - Master was not at home. It now rained most mercilessly. From the head of Loch Rog, we travelled about four miles to Luachar over a very wet and soft flat. In this course we saw a Red Grouse, a Woodcock, and a Water Rail. The latter was found dead - We reached Luachar in the dusk, weary and wet. Miss MacDonald had a headache.

Yesterday we slept till ten. The day was good, but as the ladies were fatigued we did not set out for North town. I learned that, my Water Rail had been killed by a child some days ago, and left on the moor - Rory of Kinrezort killed two deer for us, a very fine stag & a small doe. About twelve o'clock Mr MacNaughton, who had come after us today, accompanied us to the hill. But we saw no game, and returned about sunset. In the evening I recited some poetry to Miss MacDonald in the little house - Mrs Mary was snoring for part of the time. This was the first time I had completely broken that sulkiness which had oppressed me for upwards of a week. I am told I have been too cynical of late, and too imprudent in expressing my opinion, when it was not necessary. I own it: but I have only spoken truth. Truth and politeness, can scarcely agree perfectly. But if they do not live peaceably together, I shall certainly expel politeness, and become a plain honest man. "An honest man's the noblest work of God." pooh! I deny it.

Sunday, 2nd November, 1817.

We have been kept here by the badness of the weather. On Wednesday night when in bed we had three very vivid flashes of lightning accompanied by the most terrific peals I ever heard. On Friday & Saturday, I traversed part of the shooting ground without success. Yester evening I heard two sublime peals of thunder - The pleasure they afforded was of a nature not entirely new to me. Every awful object in nature yields sensations resembling this. Our situation has become disagreeable - a dirty and smoky house, conviction of having become troublesome, bad humour, want of books, & in fact of any suitable employments render the time tedious. Eagles are very numerous here. The Snow Bunting is frequently met in the hills in small flocks. I am told they are never seen in summer. I have seen the Woodcock several times - and my uncle saw another of the Water Rail kind. The weather has been boisterous with much rain and hail for upwards of a week - the mountains are tipped with snow. At Luachar is a good fishing stream; twenty barrels of salmon being caught each season upon it. The lakes in the vicinity are well stocked with trout. The salmon trout (sea trout) abounds, Ptarmigans are found in the hills. The Water Ouzel (Dipper) I saw upon the river - Ducks of different kinds, Scarts, gulls and Herons frequent the loch.

Northtown, Tuesday, 4th November.

On Monday about eight o'clock we left Luachar. About eleven we reached Miavag, and about twelve left that place. The wind was still pretty high - When we had proceeded about a mile we were obliged to take down the sails, as the wind came in squalls from the hills of Luskentir. The ladies were terrified, and we landed them at Ard Ghreotinis. After this we rowed to opposite the ford of Luskentir, and then hoisted the sails. The sea broke tremendously on the shores & rocks and as we became apprehensive that the Ford of North town could not be entered, we put about, and after a tug landed on the beach at Torgibost. Night fell before we reached North town. Today we set out on horseback for Luskentir, with the intention of carrying home the ladies. On our return we learned that the storm had been most violent - that a boat had been lifted into the air, shattered in pieces, and scattered and that several houses had been unthatched. I found a letter partly from Mr Shand, and partly from Mr Craigie. I should have been kinder to Mr Shand when here.

Thursday, 6th November

It rained for the greater part of yesterday - It having cleared however in the evening, I felt impatient of my confinement, and so putting on Uncle Toby's great coat, and arming me with a trusty cudgell, I rallied forth nor did I rest till I found myself seated at a blazing fire surrounded by old cronies, in MacPhaic's house at

Ob. I was told that they intended to have some fun, this being according to their calculation Halloween. So Donald fell a casting an egg, but he not succeeding, I was pressed to accept the office - I found the knack, and made the most beautiful pyramids and aerial bullet they ever saw. The Piob Mhor was set up, and two couples placed upon the floor. I danced five very long reels, till I was covered with perspiration. About eleven o'clock the company which consisted of a few lads and girls and old wives dispersed, and we sat down to a furious pot full of potatoes and cuddies. Upon these & milk I supped - and about twelve departed. Donald and Angus accompanied me as far as the stream - some flashes of lightning by the way. A fine starry night - wind westerly and gentle - good road. They were asleep at North town when I got there. After supper at MacPhaic's house, I was treated with a literal translation of parts of my Journal. I was astonished. Miss Marion had been so imprudent as to reveal the whole to Donald - and it even appeared that the whole Trio had read my papers. I looked silly in my own eyes. Today the weather was bad, so I could not get out. In the evening it having cleared a little I took a walk with Mrs Mac and Miss MacDonald. Traigh-na-clibhadh was the place of action - a dusky evening - the west streaked with purple - the sea agitated - high water, weeds on the beach. I was out of humour all the fore part of the day, under the influence of last night's news. I got merry however before night. Today I wrote a letter to my friends at Aberdeen. Today I saw four Starlings on the back of a horse - they appear about the houses in great flocks, often sitting upon black cattle and sheep. They are almost always to be found with the former, gathering their food among the dung.

Monday 10th, November.

On Saturday afternoon I rode to Nisbost for a book which I had lent to Mr Torrie. On my way home I called at Borve. The tide was so high upon the sand as to reach my knees. At night I read part of the Pleasures of Hope to the ladies, and engaged with Miss MacDonald not to appear out of humour all the ensuing week.

On Sunday I rose early - drank some warm milk at the gate of South town, took a walk upon Traigh na Clibhadh and Ui - during which I gathered specimens of the shell which is so common in sandy ground and of a stone formed by concretion of sand, and determined the propriety of thanksgiving, and the impropriety of the slightest deviation from truth even in a jocular way. Through the day, I took two walks with the ladies and my uncle to Bunanosh. Miss McDonald told me at bed time that I had been a good boy - & I felt the ease of having a clear conscience.

Today I rose early, drank warm milk at the gate as yesterday - then walked along the shore of Tastir, over Traigh-na-clibhadh, and along the rocks to the upper end of Moll-na-h-Uidhadh, then crossed Ui to the great sand, and returned along its margin. In this course the birds seen were the Starling, among the cattle and in the corn-yard, the Shag on the coast, the Common Gull in South town and on Ui, the Great Black-backed Gull on Moll-na-h'Ui, the Curlew on Ui in large flocks, the Wren on the marsh dyke of Ui, the Meadow Pipit on the shore, the Hooded Crow on Ui, the Raven on Fastir, and the Ringed Plover on the sands - Of other animals I saw the Homo sapiens stealing milk from some females of the Bos taurus species (cow) and in another place chasing the Equus caballus (horse). The Ovis aries(sheep) occurred also.

I have determined to describe all the birds found in Harris & shall fall to work immediately. In the evening I went to Moll to search the shores for shell-fish.

Wednesday, 12th November.

Yesterday rose early - drank milk - The weather was coarse - In the evening, it having cleared, I walked with the ladies on Traigh-na-Clibhadh - Today rose early - drank milk - the weather was good, but I had no ammunition, and was obliged to sit in the house. I manufactured a fishing line, and some nooses for small birds. Tonight I got some powder and shot, and shall in consequence commence the slaughtering business tomorrow. The description of birds should be made in the following order. Name, (Linnaean, English, Gaelic) Description proper, very minute. Bill, feet, irides, general colour, dorsal, sternal, colours, habitation, migration, nuptials, nidification, ovation, incubation, education, food, use. Bill, dimensions, colour, shape, nostrils, tongue, shape, colour, mouth colour, eyes, appendages - feet, legs, shape, colour &c. toes number, nails.

Wednesday, 20th November.

On Thursday morning, I sallied forth with my tube - after drinking milk at the gate, as usual, I proceeded to the old church & returned. In South town I shot a Pigeon and Throstle (thrush), and in the corn yard five Starlings. On Friday morning I numbered in the small bay of the Temple 105 Scarts in one flock. After breakfast, I went to Mas-na-beinnadh, attended by Domhnull ban mac Thormoid 'ic Ioin bhain.

I got no birds although I fired several shots. The birds seen were the Raven, Shag, Common Gull, Great Black-backed Gull, Turnstone, Meadow Pipit, and Woodcock. At Buninosh I shot a Snow-bunting - On arriving at the house, I found Donald Campbell of Tarinsay at dinner with the family - So - How do you do, Mr Campbell? and sat me down and snapped a hearty meal. On Saturday evening Mr Campbell departed. On Sunday the weather was fine in the morning, but rain came on before twelve - We went to Scarista to hear Master Lachlan preach. Before the service was ended the rain began to fall in torrents - So Uncle Toby had to carry Mrs & Marion through the rivulet at Little Scarista, which had got knee deep, while I carried Miss Mcdonald. So, after this Mr Lachlan was seated on horseback, and the ladies and I in cart bottom - while my uncle walked, and thus we got home. The evening passed very agreeably. On Monday the weather was coarse, so Mr Lachlan did not care about going home. In the evening I wrote some particulars regarding some birds. The wheels of life ran smoothly today. On Tuesday Mr Lachlan went home - I shot a specimen of the Reed Bunting, and described the Starling, Stock Dove, and Song Thrush. In the evening I walked on our favourite beach with the young ladies - moonlight - keen, high north wind - clouds - at intervals clear sky with stars - agreeable conversation - aye, the utmost freedom of speech, and familiarity within the bounds of reason and propriety - Today the weather has been good. Before day light I was upon Ui with my gun in expectation of falling in with the Geese some of which I had heard last night. I saw none however.

Friday, 22nd November.

Did not rise today till nine. This proved a most delightful day. After breakfast I went to South town with my gun, chased a flock of pigeons, and another of oyster catchers without success, traversed Ui, and returned about three empty-handed. The birds I saw on this excursion are the Stock Dove, Oystercatcher, Cormorant, Curlew, Raven, Hooded Crow, Meadow Pipit. After dinner my uncle and I went to Ui to look after the geese, which come there under night. The moon was shining in a cloudless sky - We did not see any however - We returned with the shepherd who met us, while I proceeded, thinking to fall in with the geese about Maclellan's park - Plovers and Snipes were whistling and rising about me in great numbers. I also fell in with several ducks and a flock of Curlews, and heard the Ringed Plover, and a bird whose note resembled that of the Redwing - no geese, however, were seen or heard, so I returned - and seating me by the table at which the young ladies were working, read the article Anger in the Encyclopaedia Britannica, and afterwards at the request of Miss Mcdonald, the Pleasures of Hope - I then played an air or two upon the Flute - and seating myself by the fire, began to prattle very much like a parrot. In the middle of my familiarity, I began jocularly to take off the fair sex - Miss Mcdonald determined not to speak a word more to me for three days! but soon broke her resolution - this induced me to repeat my quizzing. "Frailty, said I, thy name is Woman" - This determined her again and in despite of every effort held out till bed time. Between eleven and twelve I walked with Mrs McG who took this opportunity of describing a complaint with which she has been troubled for many months. It is Hysteria originating in a disordered state of the uterus, and will probably be difficult to remove, as she is naturally nervous, and as the medicines most proper for her condition cannot be obtained in this country. I have omitted that in the dusk before dinner I took a delightful walk with the young ladies nearly as far as the march of Drimafuinnd. We talked i.e. Miss Mcdonald and I for Miss Marion never speaks on these occasions, on various topics - particularly once on a horse shoe - though that for fun - for in general we are pathetic!

Sunday.

Yesterday the weather was rainy - upon getting up I knocked at the door of Miss Macdonald's bedroom - 'Don't come in - whoever you are.' Of course she had broken through her resolution. Yet perhaps this was not a fair trial. So I tormented her in various ways all forenoon - at last putting my hand upon her knee, I asked, "Are you very angry?" "Indeed I am," said she. I was overjoyed and she to appearance ashamed - for she covered her face with her hands, and after a little stay went out. In a short time she returned but still persisted in refusing to speak - However, who should come to the house, in the evening, but Messrs Stewart and McKinlay with my uncle who had gone to Rodell in the forenoon. So among the healths mine was drunk by Miss Mcdonald - and liberty of speech was again resumed.

Today the wind was high. Nothing, almost, remarkable occurred. I read part of the article America in the Encyclopaedia, and wrote a letter to my Aberdonian friends. After dinner I took a walk with the ladies on Ui - The night was stormy, but the moon shone very clear. (12 o'clock at night) It blows a hurricane - The wind from the west comes in furious blasts, with intervals of calm -

Saturday.

On Monday I went to Rodell on horseback, with the intention of procuring some medicines from Degraves - He, however, honest saxon! had left the place early for Tarbert - and although he had directed me to go down this day, had not left any thing for me. Leaving my horse in John Macdonald's square, I went to Strond and procured some sermon books from Master Lachlan's wife - After finishing my business at Rodell, I set out about three o'clock. In the Bishop's, a new name we have given Armiger, garden I saw two or three Reed-buntings. The wind blew hard in my teeth, and a prodigious shower of hail terminating in snow, attacked me with 'furious ettle'. My fingers and toes were benumbed - I got home however in tolerable condition.

On Tuesday, upon emerging from among the bed clothes I beheld the side of the hill thinly covered with snow. But as I had no powder, I made no havoc among the feathered tribes - In the afternoon I walked solus on Traigh na clibhadh, amusing myself with running, whirling, hop-step - and leaping, and spouting poetry. In the evening I accompanied the young ladies to Scarista, enjoying the pleasure of lifting them over the ford. At Scarista I got half a pound of powder - Before we returned the tide had risen, so I carried Miss Mcdonald over. I was meditating an expedition to be performed next day - But the badness of the weather on Wednesday prevented me from setting out - On Tuesday I saw a Water Rail in Allt-an-Liuir. This day I shot three Linnets before breakfast - I then set out for the hills. Above Drimafuinnd I fired at a wren, but missed - I then proceeded to the Spàg of Loch-na-morchadh, where while I was chasing a wren I observed a bird in the water making for the shore. I lay down among the heath near the water's edge, and as the bird was passing, about ten yards off I fired - but did not kill. It appeared to be the Moorhen. On my firing, it did not fly - but dived and betook itself to the opposite side, where, I believe it landed - but my search proved ineffectual. Proceeding along the water's edge I walked round the eastern extremity of the lake, without seeing any other birds than two snipes. Two blackbirds and heron occurred on the Southern side of the lake. On approaching the mill I observed Donald MacPhaic working. So I went up to him - while I was smoking here - who should come up but Rob Sinclair - as he was going to Machar, we went together as far as Creag-camna. In the evening my uncle and I played Backgammon. On the preceding evening I had lost my watch, and gained three shillings. This night I lost both watch and money - when Miss

Mcdonald had the goodness to lend me three shillings. So I played on, and lost these & three more of hers. I must remember her kindness - for she was as determined to oblige me, that she even offered her earnings when I had nothing more to stake. Supper however put an end to the diversion for the present, but after it was dispatched I got two shillings more from Miss Mcdonald, and setting to work in good earnest, recovered the whole sum I had lost - viz - nine shillings, which together with a half crown piece of Mrs MacG's which I also gained & Miss McD's two shillings made in all 13/6d. So that I had just gained 2/6 and last night 3/-. About one o'clock we gave up the job and went to bed. But, by the powers! I had almost neglected to notify a very extraordinary adventure of Nial Mac Thormid bhan's this night. About nine o'clock, by moonlight, he had been going upon some errand to the kiln, and was just entering when a figure in white appeared by his side. He stood stupefied for a moment or two, when the creature disappeared - nor could he tell in what direction it had gone. He had alarmed the whole kitchen with his story, and I am sure few of them will venture much out of doors by night for some time. It was at length settled that it must have been a Taithis. - This day was rainy from twelve o'clock -

Yester morning was occupied in making preparations for an expedition to Luskentir - On the seduction of which the two young ladies are bent: i.e. to speak plainly, Miss Mcdonald appears to look on Mr McFarlane with a favourable eye. I presume she would not be displeased at finding she had made a conquest of him. About half past twelve we set out - As we had not a woman's saddle Miss McDonald rode on my uncle's one - Donald bàn, our gillie, rode upon another horse, which we were taking, that we might accoutre him with Mrs Bethune's saddle. Marion and I walked - In this manner we trudged along till we came to the march dyke of Scarista, where I observed four curlews - in consequence of which I loaded my piece and went in pursuit. At length after a long chase I contrived to break the leg of one! At Borve I conversed with Mr Bethune in his bed room, He was very weakly, and had no hope of getting better soon. After two we set off. Myself and Miss Marion on one horse, and Miss McDonald on another - We had not proceeded far when Miss Marion fell off - and at Stà as we were descending a 'perpendicular hill' the saddle came upon the horse's neck and we were precipitated to the ground. We both lighted on our humps, clinging together very lovingly - and I finding myself not in the least hurt, could not help laughing very heartily. Yet I enquired after my companion's sanity - but she had escaped without serious damages. The mending of the girth, which had broken employed us for a quarter of an hour - Night was coming on apace - the skies lowered - and drops of rain fell - nor could we quicken our pace for fear of a second precipitation. When near Nisbost we were informed that the tide was upon the sand of Luskentir - the rain too fell in torrents, and the night promised to be sulky - so - what could we do? To return to Borve would be to disgrace ourselves. To proceed would be to be drowned either from above or from below. Mr Torrie's house lay in our present latitude: but since my uncle's marriage Mrs Torrie had cast out with him on Mrs Mac's account - Yet the ladies agreed among themselves to proceed to it - So after arriving at the door, I was appointed harbinger, and in virtue of my office, went in and saluted the good people, adding that I was very sorry I had been obliged to trouble them with the company of two young ladies -Miss McDonald and Miss McCaskill, I suppose, said Mr Torrie - 'Oh! they are extremely welcome.' So we entered, shifted, and sat down quite in a snug way to a good fire. After tea, for we got no dinner, Miss McDonald and I played at Backgammon. During part of the time occupied in this, and in playing at Drafts, I took occasion to pay a great number of barefaced compliments to my fair antagonist which she pretended not to relish very well, though she did not get angry upon it. After a great deal of giggling, we retired severally to bed - Miss McDonald's lip was swelled - she was in consequence very much afraid that her charms would scarcely be sufficient to captivate Master Mac -

Today, we got up about nine. I and Donald bàn went to the marsh, where we chased ducks and coots without success - on our way back, we fell in with the ladies - Good morning etc - Breakfasted on tea, barley-bread, salted butter, cheese and fresh beef - and set out about twelve - At two we reached Luskentir - and about an hour after I made my departure. At the marsh of Nisbost I fired at some coots, and wounded one - but did not get it. At Borve I spoke to Mrs Bethune at the door - and was not intending to enter, but Miss Bethune pulled me in. I dined here, and went to see Kenneth Morrison's wife who had a swelling of the parotid gland - At dark I departed - The rain fell pitilessly till we got home - After again dining, and shifting, and smoking, I played eight games at Backgammon with Mrs Mac - of which I gained five. After this sitting by the fire in an arm-chair I indulged a little in meditation. What is Reason! said I - in such a world of perplexity and doubt, can we be blamed if we follow the light of Revelation even if we entertain doubts concerning the authenticity of that revelation when we find it consonant with reason? No to be sure. From henceforth then, I embrace the Christian Religion as the only one that can yield me consolation during my weary pilgrimage through life -

The birds seen on this occasion were the Skylark, Meadow Pipit, Wren, Song Thrush, Common Gull, Great Black-backed Gull, Heron, Oystercatcher, Curlew, Turnstone, Coot, Raven, Mallard, and some others. I observed the Gulls on the sand of Luskentir rise to a considerable height with cockles, which they dropped in order to break them - their descent after the shell was beautiful - being performed headlong & with great rapidity.

Sunday.

Rose about eleven - the weather was good, but we did not stir from home. I was occupied for a considerable time today and last night in manufacturing an alphabet for private memoirs. This was suggested by some depredations lately committed upon my Journal by Miss McDonald.

Monday.

Today the weather was very fine - We had gone to Pabbay were it not that we wished just to go to Copay, and the badness of the sea prevented us from visiting the latter island. I cleaned my gun, and went to South town, but killed nothing. After dinner my uncle and I played at Backgammon, and did not think of giving up till we were told it was one o'clock - at which time I was eighteen games in advance. To morrow I must look about me. If at home I promise to myself to collect three species, and for this purpose, though it is now two o'clock, shall be up at dawn -

Tuesday.

It was nine o'clock before I got up today! The weather was fine at this time, but the badness of the sea prevented me from going to Copay - After breakfast I went to Moll with my gun in search of Oystercatchers - Here I saw several flocks of the following species i.e. Oystercatcher, Curlew, Turnstone, and Golden Plover but could not get near the others. In the evening, I returned by the shore - at Bunanosh I entered upon the sand, and travelled along the creek to near Ui, where I was overtaken by Donald MacCuish, breathless and reeking hot. He had been at Moll in pursuit of me, that I might reduce a dislocated arm which one of his brothers had got a little before by a fall from a horse - so we made all possible expedition. Upon arriving at Drimafuinnd I found the boy, John, (about nine years of age) sitting by the fire with a pallid countenance. His right arm was dislocated at the elbow joint outwards and backwards i.e. the lower head of the os humeri lay before the upper head of the ulna, which was also pushed to the outer side of the humerus - I did not remember to have read of this dislocation, and had never seen one reduced. But I thought that by considering the figure and connection of the bones I might succeed in reducing it. The internal condyle projected considerably as did the olecranon on the opposite side - The arm allowed motion in a rotatory manner. By pulling and twisting the forearm, I after some excition got the arm to its natural situation, excepting that the joint had not fitted, i.e. I got the olecranon removed from the external condyle, on the back part of which it lay, to near the internal one. Then after allowing it for a few minutes to remain in this position, till I got two splints made, and wrapt up in wool. I adapted a handkerchief to the projecting end of the olecranon, bending the arm gently - An assistant pulled at this handkerchief, while I with my thumbs pushed the lower head of the humerus backwards, and assisted the antetraction of the forearm. In this manner the joint was fitted with very little pain to the boy, though indeed he had suffered much during my first efforts. There was a considerable degree of swelling anterior to the joint, and where the lower head of the humerus had projected, a circular red spot. This had been the seat of intense pain - the arm was secured with two splints, and some handkerchiefs, and cold water applied to the part & directed to be kept poured at intervals through the night. Donald accompanied me, on my return, as far as the march dyke on Ui, with a horse and saddle, as before this time it had got dark - He informed me that immense flocks of the Brent goose were now at Ensay, and promised to send me word when he should kill another that I might have an opportunity of examining it. Some years ago his father used to make about £2 a year by their skins, the rate of sale being about 12/- a skin - After dinner I played at Backgammon with Uncle Toby, and was worsted by one.

Friday.
On Wednesday I saw the boy - He was without headache or heat. Pulse moderate, the arm was considerably swelled and red upon the inner condyle - cold affusion directed to be continued.
On Thursday the weather was rainy & boisterous - At 12 o'clock I began to put

in practice a plan which I had formed last night and of which an improved coition is subjoined - At Bunanosh I shot a Snipe, and proceeded nearly as far as Amhin Laidhnis, and again returned by the shore without shooting any thing, though I had seen flocks of the Golden Plover, Oystercatcher, Curlew, and Turnstone. On returning I shifted, and took a description of the Turnstone from the two specimens shot a few days ago. After dinner I played a few games at Backgammon with Mr and Mrs, transcribed three tunes, made a model of the cas-dirach (straight spade), and cleaned my gun.

General plan of conduct to be adhered to till the 1st January - To rise before, or with the sun - then to wash my face, ears & mouth. Breakfast moderate. Dinner hearty, supper light - A plan of conduct for the day to be drawn up each morning, at which time these regulations are to be read. In the evening reflections to be passed upon my conduct, and Grace to be said after meals - Penknife, inchmeasure, pencil or pen & ink and paper to be always found in my pockets - I am to be constantly on my guard against the vices mentioned below, and always anxious to put the virtues in practice - My journal is to be written regularly - never to be delayed for a longer space than thirty hours - a small bag for holding animals, birds, shells & c to be made & carried in my excursions. Notes on the subjects of enquiry to be taken down when occasion presents - for this purpose paper is always to be carried and small manuscripts kept - No opportunity of collecting specimens to be neglected. Nothing of importance to be undertaken without consideration - I must never sport with anything pertaining to Religion - must avoid disputes upon religious subjects, in fact disputes in general.

Virtues - Piety, Inviolable regard to truth, Honesty, Candour, Disinterestedness, Benevolence, Generosity, Gratitude, Punctuality, Love of order, Resolution, Patience, Perseverance, Good nature, Humility, Independance. Vices - Cursing, swearing, Insolence, Irregularity of every kind, particularly in fulfilling promises.

According to Mr Lachlan, Rooks are seen in Hirta in snowy weather - He says he once saw a Peacock there! and that it remained for a considerable time upon the stubble lands. The Solan Goose (Gannet) migrates from October to March - This & most of the birds killed for food or feathers in Hirta lay only one egg. Master Lachlan however is not good authority - as his story of the Peacock might convince one.

Friday.
Rose a little after the dawning - washed my face and mouth in the streamlet near

the house, transcribed my plan of conduct, and fulfilled its injunctions for the morning - Then made up my plan for the day, and took a description of the Snipe from the one killed yesterday. After breakfasting, I took my gun agreeably to pre-determination, and strolled over to South town, where I chased gulls, pigeons and oyster-catchers without success. The weather was cold with a north west wind, and large showers of hail - proceeding along the shore till I reached Feadan Bhallaidh, I searched for birds, and fired at a flock of oyster-catchers but killed none - I then began to ascend, and crossed the hill above Liuir - I then struck down to Moll where I fell in with oyster-catchers - but they are so shy that I begin to despair of getting a specimen. On returning I took a warm and a smoke, and after reading one of Walker's Sermons went to Drimafuinnd. The boy was well as I could wish - not a single bad symptom had occurred - the arm was swelled, but the inflammation did not appear to be violent - the swelling being in part odematous. I loosened the bandaging, and removed one of the splints, directing cold water to be still kept constantly applied. After dinner played half a dozen games at Backgammon - transcribed two tunes, played on the fiddle, smoked Tobacco, repeated some verses, thought of William Craigie and Helen MacFarlane and sighed. After supper I played again at Backgammon with Uncle Toby - and about one went to bed.

Saturday.

Was a little behind the stated period in rising - The wind was northerly and piercing - the hills are tipped with snow - I followed the injunction of my plan - But little or nothing of importance was done - only I got my hair cut. In the evening I read a sermon -

Sunday.

Rose today about eight - Drank milk at the gate of Bunanosh, returned - read a sermon, and breakfasted. About twelve my uncle went to Borve while Mrs Mac and I took a walk by Moll na h'Ui. While near this place we observed, and were soon approached by the master of Degraves's vessel, and a most insignificant creature of a painter employed by Mr Macleod of Harris in assisting to repair his house at Rodill. We went to the house with them, as they had come on a message to my uncle. In the evening they set off, and my uncle returned with the young ladies. In the course of the evening I read two sermons, my uncle one, and Mrs McG. a chapter of the bible and two psalms.

Monday.

Rose about eight - drank milk at the gate of Bunanosh - breakfasted & set out for the island of Copay. We could not effect a landing owing to the roughness of the sea. About one o'clock we reached the sand of South town after returning. About two I set out for Rodell on horseback - & reached in the dusk - I betook me to John McLeod's where I dined. After transacting some business of my uncle's, I went to Degraves's to deliver a letter. I there drank tea, and a glass of wine, & got some medicines for Mrs McG and the perusal of two books for myself; Bakewell's Introduction to Geology, and De Luc's Geology. Before I got ready, the night was considerably advanced, so accoutering me with an old great coat tied on with a bent rope, and fixing my books within my coat I mounted - The night was dark as ink, with a northerly wind, & great showers of rain - I reached however in perfect safety about ten o'clock - I was in a manner obliged to tell a lie tonight. I had been directed to get 24/- from Donald Ferguson. So I got a pound note, and took a pound of gun powder, and four of shot for the remaining four shillings. The shot I lost on the way through a hole in my pocket, so I told that I had only got the note. The balance, however, I shall contrive to pay, as soon as possible. The loss of the shot was a most tormenting occurrence - as there is none in the country.

Tuesday.

On rising I found the ground covered with hail. It however dissolved when the sun rose - but the hills continued covered all day. The wind is northerly, and the frost tonight very keen - I have been busy today in making a pair of trousers. In the morning I adhered to my plan, and in the evening took a walk on the sand where I ran and capered and leaped with great glee - and moreover carried home a mineralogical specimen.

Thursday.

Yesterday I took a walk with my gun, and fired at some curlews and larks without killing - I was delighted with the appearance of an annulus of smoke consequent to one of the shots - The rest of the day was occupied in making my trousers - Today I slept rather long - the snow continues thinly covering the ground - the frost is intense - Today the shepherd killed a small seal at Bunanosh, in describing which I was occupied for a considerable part of the day. In the evening I finished Bakewell for the first perusal, and looked over part of Linnous's mineralogy - I have deviated from my plan in neglecting the writing of yesterday's notes, in the proper time - and in omitting to read it for two or three mornings - In other respects however I have been pretty adherent.

Friday, 12th, December

Rose a little after eight, fulfilled the injunctions of my plan, and went to Copay with my uncle and four of a crew. On our outward passage I admired the beauty of the clouds in the west, and marked with delight the lofty swell of the Atlantic which at one time raised us to a considerable height, at another hid us so low under the summits of the waves, that the adjacent islands Copay and Shelay were hid from our sight. Some Scarts, gulls and a few small birds only were seen in the island - of which I killed none. On our way home we passed by the rock of Liuir and along the shore, when I took occasion to think of the formation of those steep cliffs which bound the sea over the greater part of the shore of Bencapval. The sea appears on first consideration, to be totally inadequate to form such a barrier to its own waves - and the caverns formed in many places indicate some convulsion, but on the other hand were these rocks not formed by the action of the waves, how could they almost exclusively occupy the line of coast - and that too in many places so extensively. Again the whole country has the appearance of having been inundated, and only the higher mountains and hills remaining - the former forming the larger, the latter the smaller islands. I must for the present desist from noting remarks on the appearances exhibited in the country, on account of my deficiency in mineralogical knowledge. On returning I chased some pigeons at Bunanosh without success, then crossed the ford and walked along the shore to near Scarista - on the sand I found some shells and returned. Almost every object in nature may afford pleasure to a mind adapted to receive it from the contemplation of her phenomena. Here was a sand about a mile in length - the part along the shore was in a manner separated from the rest by a mound formed by the action of the waves, from which there is a gentle declivity to the sea at low water. The whole line of coast along this sand forms a segment of a circle. The sand on which I walked was hard - the tide retired, leaving a space of about a hundred yards in breadth, secluded as it were from the rest of the country - The waves broke pretty high - the distant mountains, separated by the sea which was gently agitated, were tipped with snow - the sun was setting - crimson fleeces were floating in the west - an immense cloud in the south showed all the tints between a bright purple and milk white. The rays of the setting sun tinged the white summits of the mountains with pale crimson - all combined afforded the idea of placid serenity - I returned in the evening - cut open the eyes of my seal of yesterday, and part of the heart with the view of searching for the foramen ovale. After dinner I read part of De Luc's treatise on Geology, which I relish much, but the prattle of the ladies obliged me to give it up. In dissecting the heart I was completely disappointed, having found no traces of a foramen ovale. Yet I am inclined to think it might have been open, as I found a communication between the auricles - but I had so botched it, that I have no certainty of its existence. The sky is clear tonight, the frost continuing. The Aurora borealis in the fore part of the night appeared like an uniformly luminous zone - at present it presents the figure of a flake lying in the north west without apparent motion.

Pabbay of Harris, Monday, 15th December

I left North town on Saturday morning in a boat belonging to this island. My uncle accompanied by Miss McDonald shortly after set off in his own barge. The weather was fine - the sea smooth. I had a fine view of the sun rising over the Cullin hills in Skye, which being enveloped in gray mist presented a huge mis-shapen mass to the eye. We landed in the island of Ensay, where I took a stroll. Here I saw a very large flock of Barnacle Geese. There was a considerable quantity of cast weed upon the beach at the end of the west sand - among it I saw large flocks of Turnstones. Rock Pigeons, Curlews, and Plovers also occurred in flocks, but I shot nothing. I observed a very regularly stratified piece of rock upon the west side of the island, where I met Duncan McLellan. On leaving Ensay, we steered directly for Pabbay, where we arrived in about an hour, the wind being fair and brisk. The evening was spent without any remarkable occurrences, excepting that I was desired to visit a poor young woman who was very ill with hysterics - apoplectic symptoms. To add to the difficulty of treating her case, she was far advanced in pregnancy. I bled her from the arm.

Yesterday the weather was boisterous. Norman and my brother's teacher, Alexander Ferguson, a good sort of a blunt lad, and I took a walk by the shore, to the point near Kirktown, where we found a few small pieces of pumice. Norman says that about twenty years ago he could have gathered in a day upwards of a peck of them. They were found among rounded pebbles, at a little distance above high water mark - but have been either picked up or blown or washed away - particulars regarding this I omit at present. After visiting some sick people we returned - The evening was spent without religion.

To day I rose about nine & took a walk to Old-castle with Master Paddy, Norman's dog. After breakfast walked over the island and made some observations. In the evening I went into the Brew-house where Mr Norman was busy. Here I smoked some Tobacco, drunk some wash and some whisky - and learned the method practiced in distilling whisky over the country - Mrs McGillivray and I spoke upon particulars regarding our family to an early hour.

Tuesday, 16th December.

After breakfast I went out with my gun, and proceeded to Linach, where I picked up some mineralogical specimens. The rain began to fall, and before I had reached Kirktown by coasting I was drenched. After dinner I went to Learadh - cove to see a lad with a sore leg, and again to Kirktown to visit some sick people. On returning I smoked and drank in the Brew-house as last evening. Mr McNiel has been conversing with me, on various subjects especially on Second Sight. He says that very few are to be found now who make any pretensions to it - but that fifty years ago many were said to possess the faculty. As a proof of its reality, he mentioned the following circumstance, though I believe he has not the courage to avow his belief in it. Being once in company with other Harris gentlemen, on a visit to Macleod of Macleod, in Skye, he was sent for along with the rest to the house of a gentleman of his acquaintance. The discourse falling upon the second sight, the landlord observed that he had been very incredulous in his younger days - but had since found reason to become less sceptical. The following proof in particular, tended much to remove the prejudice he had formed against a belief in this wonderful faculty. Having once met a man of his acquaintance said to be possessed of it - he began to deride him, as had been customary with him. The man showed the utmost indifference, observing that it was a faculty more to be shunned than desired, and that he could have no incitement in such a case to make a show of what he did not in reality possess. The other desired him to predict some future event and promised in case of its fulfilment - never again to torment him. Accordingly he was informed that a burial would soon pass that way from his own house, that he should follow on horseback and that four men whom he knew, and who were named should take the bier at a particular place. Soon after a poor old man on the farm died. Being an old dependant, the gentleman was at the expense of his interment. On the day of burying, he followed in the procession determined to prevent by every mean in his power, the fulfilment of the prediction. On the way to the burial ground, a man called upon him to speak a few words - He could not refuse, though intent upon his purpose - and though the conversation did not continue five minutes - before it was ended, the men had appeared and seized upon the bier. This family has suffered great changes since last year. The Major's family has removed to Stornoway - Mrs Hutchinson is defunct - Yet if I were disposed to moralise I could find as good a text as this in almost every place, and at almost every time.

The island of Pabbay is in figure composed of an irregular low cone, half encircled with a crescent of low ground. The conical part is composed of a rocky base scantily covered with short grass. The other is, as it were, added to this upon the west, south, and east sides, on the former rocky, and on the latter sandy. The soil in general is light, where best, there being very little arable land - a very large proportion of the island however is cultivated in the ridge way. The great plain formed by the sandy part was formerly the most fertile in the country, but is now a complete dessert without a trace of vegetation - This tract was in former times considerably elevated, but the constant drifting of the sand, has reduced the lower part to nearly a level with the sea, and exposed the bare rocks on the upper. On this upper part are to be seen strata of peat moss, marle, and sand - and it is in part cultivated, producing when manured with sea wrack, very good crops of Barley. Where the sand banks have been levelled, the land is gaining considerably upon the sea, but in other places it is losing as much. An islet on the south west side of the island, which is now approachable from the main one only at low water was not very long ago joined to it by an isthmus passable at all times and upwards of three hundred yards in length. Near this, strata of moss are seen under high-water mark - and on the east side of the island, Mr MacNiel informs me, are seen at very low tides, considerable pieces of moss in which are found stumps and roots of trees with the bark remaining, but so much decomposed as to prevent the distinguishing of the species. Shells are found among the sand banks as in other places of Harris. These are in common of the Limpet and Wilk (Whelk) families. The agriculture does not differ here from the system practised all over the district. The island is divided into two farms, Lingay and Balnakill or Kirktown: the former consisting of three pennies, tennanted by Mr McNiel & in part sublet; the latter consisting of four pennies, and held by a great number of small farmers or tenants as they are called by way of distinction from the Tacksmen. Each penny pays £28 yearly. So that the rent of the island amounts to £196. A stranger from a fertile country, would never deem it worth £20 if even that. The animals seen here were the Grey Seal, Otter, House Mouse, there are no rats, Skylark, Meadow Pipit, Linnet, Song Thrush, Mallard, Red-breasted Merganser, Curlew, Snipe, Turnstone, Shag, Cormorant, Golden Plover, Stock Dove, Great Black-backed Gull, Common Gull, and perhaps others.

Wednesday, 17th December.
The weather was fine till about five o'clock when it became very boisterous. After breakfast I visited some sick people, and took a walk to the west of Kirktown. The evening was occupied in reading De Luc - I have been remiss in following my plan -

Thursday, 18th, December.
The storm had subsided by ten last night. The weather today was calm but dull, with some showers. After breakfast I went to the east side of the island. Here are numerous springs of very clear water. As the sand from among which they rise is calcareous or composed of shell, I suspect the water to be impregnated, more especially as the stones in many of the rills are encrusted - At the cove of Linach I saw a large flock of pigeons and some Scarts of which two were crested. I had determined to coast round the island. On the north side the shore is rocky and in many places precipitous. A rock opposite the island of Shelay in particular engaged my attention. It is about 100 feet in height, and 600 in length. The strata appear to be nearly perpendicular in some places, as is the face of the rock though very irregularly so. Its form is semicircular or hollowed. From near its centre a ridge of rocks nearly covered at high water stretches out about 500 feet - This ridge is separated from the rock. On the west side of it is a beach composed principally of small rounded pebbles, mixed with larger. On the other side are large fragments of rock evidently debris. Both these appear heaped up against the base of the rock. Near this I saw a Woodcock. A little to the westward of this rock is a kind of cavern which presents the appearance of a fissure, half choaked up at the upper part with fragments of various sizes. The

wild pigeons in the fissures stretching their glancing necks to view me, looking peculiarly beautiful. One is pleased to find animation of any kind in such a place, but to see such beautiful birds as these he is delighted. Still further on is another rock, not high and partly removed from the sea, with a declivity at its base, terminating in a hollow - both covered with masses of rock. The next cave is on the northwest side of the island. It is indented in the rock and has a large mass in the middle at its entrance, a formation not uncommon among the caves of Harris. Here is a small cavern irregularly arched, appearing as if chizzelled out of the rock. The two sides are parallel and a little inclined from the vertical - still there was no appearance of detrition - the whole was rough and irregular. The waves presented the most tremendous appearance one could see of the kind. For a quarter of a mile out they were seen rolling in successive ridges of vast size to the shore, curling their whitening heads as they approached it. The agitation became greater as they advanced, increased by the retrograde current of each retiring wave. When these encountered they rose to a great height. This obstacle overcome, the wave rushed forward with prodigious force, dashing against the rocks and rising in one huge cloud of foam. I computed the height to which it rose on a point near at 80 feet. The roar was continuous and loud - the rocks on which I stood shook, and the mist rose like that of a cataract - While I was descending here to get a view of the cavern my powderhorn slipped out of my pocket and bounding from crag to crag was quickly buried in the waves. The next cave that occurs is singular. It is in the form of a vast fissure, the sides of which do not agree. A noise like thunder was produced by the rattling of the pebbles on its narrow floor when the wave retired. About twenty paces farther is the last cave of any note in the form of a superficial fissure. The west and south west coast appears to be full of sunk rocks and banks for more than a mile out as the sea was breaking very high to that distance. There was some tangle on the shore - the cattle feed upon it at low water, and it is said to be their chief support during the winter.

Friday, 19th December.
Norman began to tell a tale last night, after we had got to bed, as he had done for some nights past, but fell asleep before he had finished it. Today the weather was serene - I took a walk with my gun and shot a Wren. On returning I wrote a description of the Skylark, a specimen of which I had also shot. Mr McNiel of Kyles, William Mackenzie, and Murdoch McLellan came in the afternoon. They and Niel Campbell had a violent squabble about St Kilda.

On Monday I left Pabbay after promising to return that night, and leaving my papers. My friends at North town detained me however, and I have not been at Pabbay since.

North town, 6th January, 1818

I have neglected to note occurrences and observations for upwards of a fortnight, owing to my having left my Journal in Pabbay. On Saturday last I took my gun, and went to Ronaval in search of ptarmigans, but found none. I returned by the north side of Loch Languad. On Sunday I set off early for Caolas Stocnis, having heard that a large unknown animal had been found there. The weather was coarse in the fore part of the day. I left my horse in the house of Rory Macleod of Craco, where I breakfasted, and drank three or four cups of whisky. Rory himself accompanied me. It was after twelve when we got down - A great number of people from the neighbouring bays had collected to see the wonder. It was so mutilated by the fellows who killed it, that no accurate description could be taken: It had been skinned and the carcase cut into pieces. I found it to be the Trichechus Rosmarus, the Morse Walross, or Sea horse (Walrus)*. It was about the size of a bull - and two barrels of blubber were got upon it. On returning to Craco in the evening, I took some meat, and drank two cups of whisky - then mounted, and rode home - where I arrived as they were sitting to dinner at six o'clock. Yesterday was held as Christmas. Nothing very worthy of noting occurred. Today we did not rise till twelve. I sat up some hours after the rest, scrawling some lines of what I call poetry.

Wednesday, 7th January.

Rose pretty early, sent of an account of the Morse to the Inverness Journal. Breakfasted alone - shook hands with Miss Marion - mounted my horse, and rode to Nisbost. 'The Lady of the Lake', which Mr Torrie promised me some days ago was not to be found. So I returned as I went. On the way I met Mr MacFarlane, and Sandy Stewart, & Miss Bethune and the children, the former coming from Rodill, the latter bound for Nisbost, to hold the Christmas with Mr Torrie. A plan of conduct is absolutely necessary. I have had none for some time past; but let me now in my

*MacGillivray made a full description and a detailed series of measurements of this animal. An article describing the walrus, published in the Edinburgh Philosophical Journal in 1820, was his first scientific paper.

wisdom! sit down and frame one - After doing so I found it would not do - & determine to act without plan, according to the dictates of my conscience & of my religion. I promised today to give Torrie a sketch of the Morse's head.

Saturday, 10th January.

I have killed a useless horse for the purpose of shooting an Eagle or a Raven upon it. I have not yet been successful, but I probably shall next week. Tonight the Shepherd brought me an Oyster-catcher. I have formed a kind of plan for next week to which I trust I shall be able to adhere. I divide it into two classes: one relating to the body, the other to the mind-

Corporeal.

The chief object in this department is to acquire and maintain health and vigour with such a degree of hardihood, dexterity and address as may enable the machine to perform the various functions of life with ease. To attain these, the proper regulation of diet, exercise and rest is to be attended to: while the circumstances which tend to destroy life, or to vitiate the frame are to be avoided.   Diet - this article is too much at the mercy of circumstances to be adapted to its natural purpose, with strict propriety. However, little perversion is made in this country: the substances used being in general proper, though the periods are not in common judiciously chosen. All I can do is never to continue to eat till the stomach is burdened, but rather to leave off while the appetite still continues. As to Exercise: I would have it always to be rather violent than too gentle: for besides its other good effect, it will have a great tendency to banish idleness. Exercise may be combined with amusement, and even with study. It becomes subservient to the latter, when I search for mineralogical and zoological subjects: to the former when modified into running, leaping, and putting the stone; to both when I look upon the objects which present themselves during my excursions with the eye of a poet or of a philosopher. Sleep; the duration of this must be proportioned to circumstances - varying from five to seven hours. The powers most likely in this country to vitiate the constitution are cold and wet: Both are to be carefully avoided when not absolutely necessary to be endured. Too great warmth is to be shunned, as it renders the frame more liable to be acted upon by the preceding. Under this article may be ranked hot food, which destroys the tone of the stomach and spoils the teeth. Intemperance in eating has been mentioned with disapprobation. It is alike detestable and injurious under all its forms-

Mental:

This division is too extensive for a detail of its particulars. Its primary divisions are Morality and Study. At present I shall only mention those virtues which I shall most carefully cultivate. Charity, comprehending Benevolence and Beneficence. Most inviolable regard to Truth. Decency in behaviour, equally removed on the one hand from immodest action and expression, or intemperate mirth; and on the other from morosity, fretfulness, or pride. Toward my equals, let my behaviour be gentle, social, pleasing, accommodating, polite; toward my inferiors condescending, affable, humane, taking care however that I transgress not on either side. To my friends let me be all gentleness and politeness. Let it be my constant endeavour to diffuse happiness around Perseverance, Resolution, Firmness. I have often allowed an erroneous opinion to pass unnoticed, because I was too diffident. But let me never be ashamed or afraid to be an advocate for the Truth. The vices or failings to be most carefully avoided are, Rudeness, Irresolution, Procrastination, Idleness. Let not a moment if possible be unemployed. It is an easy matter to find suitable employment: and let no opportunity of doing good both to myself and others be neglected or unimproved. Patience, Consideration. Let me never enter upon an undertaking however apparently inconsiderable, without previously weighing its advantages & disadvantages. Study: For the ensuing week I shall content myself with reading that part of the article Anatomy in the Encyclopaedia Britannica which treats of the bones and muscles, & the book of Job.

Wednesday, 14th January.

On Sunday I rose pretty early. After breakfasting, the ladies and I went to Scarista in a cart to hear Master Finlay preach. He did not however make his appearance. So the ladies returned; and I proceeded to Borve to visit a sick girl. After giving my advice to her, I went to Mr Bethune's where I remained all night. The evening was spent in conversation and in reciting some poetry. I retired to bed at a late hour, having occupied myself for some hours previous to incubation in reading the newspapers, and some books on religious subjects. About 4 in the morning, a boy came from North town for a saddle, I accompanied him home, where we arrived in the dawn. Ewen MacDiarmid had arrived on the preceding afternoon, and Mr MacCaskill under night.

Monday was kept as New-Year's-day in the old style. After breakfast, Miss

MacDonald, Mrs MacGillivray, and I went to Rodell on horse back: the former lady being under the resolution of leaving the country by the first packet. We were accompanied by my uncle and some others for a great part of the way. Near Cosladir, we met a lad, Mac Iain oig mhic Cuthis, with a Heron which he had shot. My uncle obtained it from him. On reaching Rodell, we visited Ch. Campbell, Stewart, and Donald MacDonald. In the house of the latter, Miss MacDonald was to be accommodated. Doctor McKinlay, and Master Finlay accompanied the ladies for a short way from the village, as we were preparing to return, while I was left behind to take care of the horses. In sooth, though I cannot entirely approve of the conduct of the ladies in this particular, especially of Mrs McGillivray, I own that I was in nowise worthy of attention in as far as regarded externals; for I was but shabbily dressed, while the other young men had very handsome habiliments. However, it behoves me not to pay too much regard to such circumstances. Mrs Mac and I mounted our horses about half past two, and reached home in the dusk. We had called at MacPhaic's house on the way to see a Cormorant which Donald had killed, and we were drenched with rain. The evening was spent in drinking, dancing, and singing. We bedded about four next morning.

On Tuesday I was called up before daylight to go to Scarista to see a boy. He had been drinking, and had been laid in bed; but was not observed to be ill till he appeared past redemption. I drank a good deal with the MacDonalds.

Thursday

Today we have had a most sublime storm which continued all day. The wind comes in great blasts succeeded by intervals of calm. The water upon the sand at high tide rising in the air by the force of the whirlwinds, presented a most beautiful phenomenon. The sea has been in great agitation: but I have been prevented by the weather from going to South town to view it in all its grandeur. Our houses were secured with ropes, and stones, and logs. Last night we had Mr MacRae and Mr McKinlay here. We drank punch all night. Mr MacRae and I entered upon a dispute about the comparative merits of the Gaelic & English languages in point of expression, which was ended apparently to the satisfaction of neither: though I own I was worsted because I had taken the wrong side. I am in a dilemma. I cannot determine whether it is better to display any little talents that I may possess to the world; or to speak merely according to the suggestion of circumstances. Why, to be sure, the latter, yet I have vanity - Yes an intolerable degree of it.

Sunday, 17th.

On Saturday the storm having abated, I went to Rodill to see Miss MacDonald who had been windbound there since Monday. I procured some shot & in the evening returned. I have improved much in riding since last year, when I could scarcely sit upon a saddle without holding by the mane. Mr MacRae and the doctor returned to Rodill on this day - They had been at North town on the preceding night. Today my uncle, Mr McCaskill, Miss Marion and I went to Scarista to hear Master Finlay preach. Donald and Archibald Stewart, and the Bethunes were there. Tonight I saw a porpoise which Aonas mac Uilleam had found upon the shore. It appeared to be the Delphinus phocona (Common Porpoise) of Linnous. I have done well within these ten days, for I have got four species of which I was before ignorant, and which are difficult to be obtained: the Oystercatcher, Cormorant, Heron, and Porpoise.

Ceann-dibig. Wednesday

Yesterday left North town in company of Mr McCaskill and Miss Marion on their way to Uig. At Scarista we drank some whisky - Called at Borve - Marion rode to the north side of the sand of Luskentir: - From that to Ardhasig she walked in my arm, at least having a hold of my hand. The weather was bad, and the mist so thick upon the hill that at times we could not see three hundred paces before us. At Ardhasig we put up in the house of a namesake of theirs, where we had an excellent fire, but a rather indifferent supper and bad beds. I amused Marion & myself with reciting poetry, and reading part of my journal, leaving the rest to entertain each other as they pleased. Mr McCaskill & the people of the house engaged in a serious conversation regarding horses, cows, oats, potatoes & herring, Lairds & tennants, Schoolmasters and scholars, and various other topics connected with the country - While, I, who have in sooth become prodigiously sentimental of late, chose rather to discuss topics of a nature more congenial to my ideas, and so seated me by the honest man's fair daughter - and by way of manifesting my attachment, laid my head upon her shoulder: for I could not hope to prevail upon her to lean upon me - So we had a long and agreeable conversation. I observed that my poetical recitations excited the wonder of the good people around the fire. In the morning Miss Marion & I took a walk - she observed that it was probably the last time we should walk together for years - but I reminded her of my promise of going to Uig to see them before my departure. On returning we breakfasted - so we parted - & I pursued my way to

Tarbert. I arrived here about one o'clock: and was very kindly received by my Bangosti, who set potatoes and herring before me of which I ate heartily. The evening was spent in hearing tales, speaking etc.

Sunday 25th January, 1818 North town.
"Man is born to trouble as the sparks fly upward."
On Thursday the weather was bad, with great showers of snow accompanied by a strong northerly wind. I left the house about eleven o'clock and travelled toward the ridge of Ben Luskentir. On a small lake near Ceanndibig I shot a beautiful little species of duck unknown to me - and not among Linnous's. Travelling onward I was nearly benumbed with cold. However I reached North town before six o'clock; and though I had been wetted in crossing the ford did not feel any other than a slight temporary inconvenience from my trip. Friday and Saturday were slurred over in idleness. Not so with Sunday - My uncle had been thinking of setting off for Inverness on Sunday morning. One of the servants sat up to prepare some linnen in the room where I slept. I chatted with her for some time after going to bed - and about three o'clock had scarcely fallen sleep when I heard Mrs McGillivray calling to the girl to look out - she had heard the cattle lowing in the byre. In less than a minute after I heard the cries of the girl, and jumping instantly out of bed, ran to the door, naked as I was - but stopped a moment to consider, returned, thrust on my trousers, and sallied forth. On turning the end of the house, a most alarming spectacle presented - the byre was completely enveloped in flames. My uncle in his shirt only was at the door. I ran to hold him - The whole interior was on fire. Three beasts were to be seen lying on their sides roasted alive - The entrails were bursting through one. It was a most melancholy sight. My uncle ran to the end of the house where he fell among the flames and burnt his hand, but I snatched him out, and followed him. Mrs McGillivray was at the end of the house half naked - they both returned as all hope of saving anything was over. I remained to assist in extinguishing the fire. Luckily the wind was not high, else the dwelling house might have shared the same fate. We knocked in the walls upon the burning materials, and covered the whole with earth, so that before day break all was secure. But this was not all - the dairy maid had fallen into a most violent paroxysm - she had a very frequent and full pulse - oppressed and interrupted breathing, and fits of spasm, alternating with short deliquiums. I bled her and applied hot water to the extremities. She recovered happily, before next

evening - but continued even then in a dangerous state - on looking today upon the ruins, I could not refrain from shedding a tear when I saw the poor Each brogach lying in the door with his pile all burnt off - Poor fellow! how often had he carried me on his back. How many happy hours have I spent with my poor but warm hearted associates, in galloping with him over the plains of Ui and the sands of Bencapval - without saddles, and with our handkerchiefs for bridles. And then so kind and docile as he was - When I fell, he would not run over me, or make his escape - He even seemed to feel pleasure in carrying me. Poor fellow! there is happiness and misery associated with thy remembrance. Oh! for the days of childhood again with all their misery, Ever shall their remembrance be dear to my heart. The social circle of poor islanders assembled round the blazing hearth, the tales of other years with all their romantic wildness, the evening excursion to catch the saithe on the rocks of South town, the watching of the wild geese on the lake of Ui. All are gone for ever - but the impression remains, and will soothe many a pang to come. Farewell my poor friend! thy span of existence is measured.

North Town, Monday - February 1818

Yea verily all is vanity and vexation of spirit. Since last report I have fared queerly - but somehow, I could not prevail upon myself to brandish a quill in the journalizing way till tonight. The heads however of the discourse which I should have written are the following: As my uncle was incapacitated by the accident which befell him from going to Inverness, I volunteered my services, which were accepted. So I went out in the packet. Mr Stewart went out also for the purpose of meeting Mr Macleod the Laird who was with his lady at Dunvegan Castle. On our arriving, Macleod of Macleod and Mr Macleod met Mr Stewart on the shore - Mr Macleod asked me dryly, "How do you do?" without shaking my hand. I went to Suardal where I remained that night. Next morning as I was preparing to set off, met Mr Stewart. He had got a letter informing him that the business upon which I was employed was transacted. So I returned two days after - We encountered a tremendous hurricane one night in the packet - But we were sheltered by an island, and were moored to the rocks by two cables - During the storm the sea all around was like a plain of drifting snow - Several of the windows of Dunvegan Castle were broken, and the lead torn from the roof. Mr Macleod, and his young wife, with a little sister of hers, and Stewart, came by the packet. I was not invited to Mr Mac's house - in fact was scarcely spoken to.

I sit up tonight - preparing for a trip to the hills of Harris and to Uig in Lewis - My motives are connected with a poem in contemplation, and with my friends in Uig & the forest. I have been pestered of late with sick people. Mr McKinlay appears to be rather unhappy in practice; and the people have taken a most insuperable dislike to him. They appear to be determined not to pay a farthing of his salary - but, poor wretches, they will be compelled. They all offer to pay it to me, with the greatest cheerfulness - many of them would even pay double rather than that I should not stay among them - but the lot is cast, and I cannot retract, though indeed I am now and then inclined to think I should have accepted the offer made by Mr Macleod. I might certainly be happy enough in a country where I am beloved by all - But let my wayward fate take its own way - I trust I am prepared for the worst. As to health - I enjoy it, thank heaven! as much as I could wish. The pains so long felt in my breast have been dissipated - The chief cause of all my disquietude is the want of resolution - and now I summon all my energy, and am determined to make one desperate effort. If my bad habits were once broken I should be happy - I should like a virtuous life - and the consciousness of integrity would assuredly support me under all my afflictions - Now for it then - one effort more.

Tuesday - 1 o'clock A.M. I have just written a letter to my friends at Aberdeen, in which I promise to make my appearance, about the 20th of March.

Luachar, Wednesday 11th.

After sitting up all last night I left North Town about six in the morning. It was not clear light till I reached Scarista. My intention in setting out so early was to get over the Luskentir sand before the tide should cover it. But before I reached it, it was completely covered. Until I got half way up Benluskentir the weather continued good, with a high wind from the South. Here however it began to rain - and the mist lay so thick upon the hill that I lost my way, and came upon the rocks of Tarcle. A little on this side of Tarbert I met Ross the Catechist, who told me it was twenty minutes after twelve. So I determined to set out for Luachar - and after passing Ardhasig held up the glen above Bun-abhin-edir. From this place to the head of Loch Languad the glen is bounded laterally by lofty mountains of a very rugged aspect - the snow lay here and there upon their sides, as well as in the glens in considerable masses - the water which from the melting of the snow fell in great quantities was perfectly clear - Nothing could appear more ridiculous than the opinion that such insignificant streams as run from these mountains could ever have formed such vast vallies - The fact assuredly is that the streams instead of having formed the vallies merely run in them from natural necessity. When about three miles from Luachar I began to grow faint - so that I was obliged to rest a dozen times before I ascended an acclivity there. When I had gained the summit night fell - and I turned so weak that my legs could scarcely support me - Luckily I had a declivity for the greater part of the way, and the moon though the sky was cloudy kept up a sort of twilight - Whenever I came among snow, or attempted to step over a bog, I always fell on my knees - though exceedingly weak, I felt no sickness, but rather a pleasantish sort of sensation - my pulse was rapid and weak - The cause of this probably was the drinking of three draughts of snowwater when warm, and upon an empty stomach. I reached Luachar however about two hours after dark; and entering the house announced my arrival by enquiring if they were going to bed yet - Mrs MacDiarmid kissed me. I have loved this family since my first acquaintance with them, and my affection is not diminishing. They have an equal regard for me. I am now shifted, and got a little spirits and meat, and sat me down most comfortably to a large fire. On the moors in this country no such thing as even ground is to be seen - The surface is always broken and intersected with bogs - so that there is no comfortable walking on them excepting in summer. The circumstance of there being streams in every valley to cross renders it still more inconvenient. I never endeavour to keep my feet dry while travelling upon them, as I know it to be impossible if the distance be great, but dash through every bog that lies in the way. This to be sure is very bad for shoes - the only kind for such travelling is that made of highland or half-tanned leather. This kind lets in water by the seam: but they also let it out when filled: and for this reason are much more comfortable than tanned ones. To add to my comfort tonight I was told that Helen and Marion promised to come here along with me on my return from Uig. After supping very heartily I bedded - As I was dry, Mrs McDiarmid had the kindness to make tea for me after I was in bed. I enjoyed a most uninterrupted sleep till about ten next day, when I woke. Today I rose about twelve. After breakfasting I went out with my gun and shot a Turnstone. A servant of Mr MacCaskill's has come from Uig today - she was the bearer of a line from the girls, in which they desire their sister to send me over immediately upon my arrival, and promise to accompany me to Luachar. Thank heaven! thought I, I shall be happy for a week at least. At present I am quite comfortable, and quite at peace with myself, and all mankind, if I except perhaps Miss McDonald! Tomorrow, if the weather admit, I shall go to Uig-

Thursday.

Though the weather was good yesterday I was so fatigued that I did not care about going to Uig. Today the weather was most boisterous with continued and heavy rain. I lay in wait for some ducks in the afternoon, but without success; and saw a flock of plovers with several Turnstones intermixed. I also saw a flock of Snowflakes (Snow Buntings) upon the shore. In the evening it cleared up, and we had a most delightful moon and star light night. About eleven I took a little walk near the head of the Loch - I recited some poetry, and just glanced at a plan of a poem - I felt the most enchanting serenity - my soul was perfectly accordant with the night. A cloudless sky, with the moon & stars & with scarce a breeze of wind - a smooth lake into which ran a mountain torrent - and a wide expanse of dark heath terminated by lofty mountains constitutes the scene. No sound was to be heard excepting that of the torrents from the hills.

Luachar, Wednesday.

On Friday, after breakfasting very heartily I left Luachar for Uig, accompanied by Mr MacCaskill's servant Katherine Macdonald, a good looking young woman, and more than this, a good one too. Though the day had been fair till now, rain began to fall, and increased till we reached Uig in the evening - I met Mr McCaskill in the door, & Misses Helen and Marion in the inner entrance, both of whom I kissed as in duty bound! I had scarcely shifted my pedicles when two fellows came in; a Mr Ross. Excise Officer, and Kenneth McKenzie, a respectable merchant in Stornoway, after that a private soldier and now holding some petty office in the civil line. The latter staid all night, the former went to Mr Munroe's. After supper I sat some hours in the little house with the girls, talking upon various subjects and making ourselves as happy as we could. In fact I enjoyed as much felicity as I could well wish - at least expect. About twelve I retired to bed - Next day I rose about ten when I breakfasted, and received an invitation from the Munroes to dine with them. In the forenoon I visited some sick people in Peinn-domhnuill, a village or farm about half a mile from Mr McCaskill's, and on returning went with Mr Mac to the minister's. Here I found a young lady, Miss Margaret Shaw to whom I was in course introduced

- She is a very tall, handsome, agreeable girl. If I be rightly informed, Mr Macrae is enamoured of her. They would make a rather oddly-matched pair. For my part I like much better to see a tall man with a little wife, than a tall woman with a mannikin; though I am better pleased still to find a naturally-matched couple, that is the man just a little taller, and a great deal more muscular than the woman. We dined upon "flesh, fowl, and fish" with soup, potatoes and bread. Our conversation was of the trifling kind. I narrated all the little stories about Harris that I could muster - the good people, from their situation in a remote corner of the island, being very keen for news of all kinds. Miss Marion was not at home. After drinking tea, we returned home - the schoolmaster took me to a tennant's house by the way, where I was obliged to remain upwards of an hour with him, much against my will, for I would much rather been hugging the honest man's daughter. However home we got at length. The evening was spent as the last.

On Sunday the weather was most delightful. In the forenoon the girls and I walked along the sea as far as Capdal, a farm about a mile and a half off. Here I spoke to some sick people, and returning visited those at Peinn-domhnuill. The servant met us to inform us that we had been sent for, to dine at Mr Munro's. He himself had gone to Bernera, a neighbouring island to preach. So we dined and drank tea with the ladies. In the evening I went, accompanied by Mr MacCaskill to visit a sick woman in Crallasta, a farm about half a mile from Balnakill, the minister's place.

Uig is one of the four parishes of Lewes. It is situated on the west and south side of the island, comprehending a large district of very rugged ground. The cultivated part lies on the west coast by the sea, and consists of a considerable number of farms lying about a sand similar to those of Ben Capval & Ben Luskentir, but of much less extent than either. There are no plains of any size: but small hills intersected by proportionate vallies - the whole rocky as in Harris. Hence the view is interrupted, excepting from an elevated station. Pretty high hills of a most rugged and bleak aspect encircle the whole at the distance of two miles or thereabouts. Belonging to this parish is an island, Bernera, of considerable extent and value. Here the minister preaches once every three weeks. The farms which I have seen are Baile-na-Cille, Drumisgarry, Erista, Baile-Nicoil, Peinn-Domhnuill, Capdal, Crallasta, Carnis. On a streamlet on the farm of Erista are seven small mills, the best of which will grind four sacks of barley or nine of oats, with five Lewes peats to the sack, in twelve hours - the worst two or three sacks of barley. I entered one of them but did not see the whole of the machinery - as there is one here of the same size I may scrutinize it - At the head of the sand is a pretty large stream, which comes from two lakes, one of which, is about two and a half miles in length. On this stream which passes through a very rugged channel forming some fine falls, is a Cruive (fish trap) belonging to Mr Munro. The larger lake is called Loch Suainnebhal - A large rugged hill at the eastern extremity of it is called Suainnebhal.

On Monday I left Uig, accompanied by the young ladies, who had obtained leave from their father with much difficulty to go to see their sister at Luachar. Their principal inducement however was to spend a few days with me before my departure. The schoolhouse is said to be nine miles from Luachar - that is, nine highland miles or twelve English. To the south end of Loch Suainnebhal the road or path is over very rugged ground. When about half way we eat a duck & some barley bread, and trimmed ourselves to meet the rain which now began to fall with fury. Night was just falling as we reached Luachar. After shifting we sat down to a vast fire, and felt very comfortable. Without pain there would not be pleasure.

Yesterday I took a walk by the loch with the girls. Today I rose pretty early - walked with the girls before breakfast - after that went with them and two children to gather mussels, of which there is abundance here, and to look for pearls. We broke some shells, and picked out a considerable number of very small pearls, which however will serve for specimens - the mussel from which they were taken is the Mytilus edulis of Linnous. We carried hence a great quantity for the same purpose. Pearls are also found in oysters, as I have been informed by Mr Simson in Lewis and my goshti in Harris. The latter tells me there are fresh water mussels in the lakes in which pearls are found.

I bathed about two o'clock in the sea, shaved, and shifted. After this I wrote these notes, and sat a while with Helen and Marion. John MacNaughton and his wife came in the evening from Loch Ròg - The house was in consequence much crowded; and we could well have dispensed with the company. After the rest had bedded the girls and I sat some hours by the fire - After talking a good deal, we read several chapters of the Bible and bedded.

Thursday.
Before I had bedded last night an eruption of small pimples had appeared on my

chin - I was sickish also, and through the night slept but uncomfortably. I rose today about ten. After breakfast the girls and I went to Toray a small farm about two miles from Luachar on the Lewes side of the Loch for the purpose of seeing a child of Ewen's kept there by Tormid ban. In his house Marion remained, while I and Nelly went to Scianaid, about a quarter of a mile farther down to see a goshti of hers. On returning we eat some barley bread and milk. It was evening before we reached Luachar. I see I must take at least two days to the mountains and glens which are to constitute the scenery of my poem. The young ladies are to return home on Saturday, and I could wish to be able to set off for North town on that day - but am afraid I cannot. I shall see however how much I can do to morrow. The plan which I have made up is this. The hero is to be introduced standing on a hill on the Lewes side of Loch Resort, making some very wild reflections. He next proceeds to Luachar where he meets his mistress. A hunting bout is proposed by the good man of the house who is to act as guide. Next day after traversing the hills and vallies they come to Glen Ulladil, where they are overtaken by a terrible storm of thunder and take shelter in the cave - The storm continuing and night coming on they determine to remain all night. This happening to be the last night of the season some troops of daoine sith are introduced, agreeably to the belief of the country people. The storm dissipating - night scene - moonlight - returning to the house of Lauchar they meet at Balla-mhic-ic-Ioin bhan a hermit who conducts them to his hut. Conversation with him. Torquil returns satisfied and delighted - Meets a messenger sent for him - parting interview with Maria at Sron-nan-Scuird - His reflections conclude the poem. This is but the plan in embryo. I may find opportunities of improving it during my peregrinations among the hills - the manners and character of the islanders are to be described, and several songs introduced.

Friday

After sitting some hours by the fire as usual, and reading some chapters of the Bible we retired to bed. I slept today till after ten. As the weather was very bad with showers of snow I did not go to the hills, but contented myself with shooting at some birds near the house. I killed a specimen of an Oystercatcher and a Curlew with one shot, and a Plover with another. Mr & Mrs MacNaughton went away in the forenoon, after I had bled the former, and given some directions in writing to the other for a stomach complaint - Both seemed much pleased with my attention to them, and at their departure besides shaking my hand most cordially wished a thousand blessings to attend me. The evening was spent in trifling, making a pair of leaden earrings for a girl, writing some directions for some sick people in Uig, sitting with the girls some hours after the rest had bedded, reading as usual, and such like. The birds seen today were two White-tailed Eagles upon a stone in the Loch, the Oystercatcher, Golden Plover, Turnstone, Starling, Skylark, Common Gull, Hooded Crow, Raven, Song Thrush, Stock Dove, and an aquatic bird unknown to me.

Saturday.
Nothing of importance occurred today. I did not stir from home, the weather being bad. The hills are covered with snow - the girls have postponed their departure till to morrow.

Sunday
I shall divide the scene into four divisions. Before me, and in the centre is the glen of Ulladil, bounded on one side by an awful rock, on the other by the craggy declivity of a mountain. The glen disappears in the distance by climbing between the mountains and above Luachar terminates in an open plain with a stream running through it to the head of Loch Resort. To the east of Glen Ulladil there is a lofty hill, the nearer part of which terminates in the rock mentioned; and on its farther shoulder is seen part of a craggy corry - A hill, or rather series of small hills gradually decreasing, and separated from the main hill by a deep valley sweeps toward the head of Loch Resort, and separates the glen already described from that of Miavag, at which commences the range of mountains which constitutes the most eastern division of my scene. Here I have a piece of highland scenery worthy of the highest admiration. Ridges, and peaks, and rocks and vallies all blended together terminating in the most eastern distance in the summit of Cliseim in the western in Sron nan Scuird a rock of at least two thousand feet in height. Through the glen is seen part of the hills of Luskentir. Still farther to the eastward the hills become smaller, and stretch away into the flats of Lewes covered with lakes and morasses - these however are not seen. From Glen Ulladil to Loch Resort is the third division, consisting of hills and vallies much more uninteresting than the former, and terminating in a high cliff forming part of the shore of the Loch - In the highlands and isles, Loch is applied to an arm of the sea as it is called, as well as to a collection of fresh water -

perhaps in description the term loch should be restricted to the former, & lake appropriated to the latter - Loch Resort, then is a long narrow arm of the sea lying north west and south east. Lastly the island Scarp, and the low hills of Lewes, between which glimpses of the Atlantic are seen constitute the fourth division. The three large vallies, Gleann Ulladil, Gleann Mhiabhag, and Gleann-a-chlair, run all together into the plain at the head of Loch Resort.

This description was taken upon the summit of a hill of no great elevation on the Lewes side of Loch Resort, from which Glen Ulladil is seen in the west, south west: The scenery described is most sublime when viewed from a considerable eminence, but loses much when viewed from the level of the sea, as the hills then appear lower and much of the vallies is hid from the eye by the intervention of eminences. The ground is all covered with heath, and interspersed with stones and rocks - No green grass, such as is to be seen in the low country is found here, excepting about the shielings to which the natives resort in summer for the purpose of making their little butter and cheese.

Today I rose about nine. After breakfast the girls prepared for their departure. I accompanied them about a mile and a half - The weather was cold with showers of snow - The hills are covered with snow. Upon a little eminence where we sat for some time we raised a small cairn of stones - My friends wept - and some drops fell from my own eyes - Dear girls! Can I ever cease to love you? No - you have soothed the pangs of a wounded spirit - you were stars to me in a land of darkness - your remembrance shall be dear to my heart. I could wish to think that I am not ungrateful - Nor am I by nature; but strange ideas occur at times; and I too often for my peace see the world involved in gloom. I kissed them, and turned away - After proceeding some way, I thought of returning to see them again, but considered that it would betray a degree of weakness which I would not be willing to own, and proceeded to Luachar. I mounted a rocky eminence however, and took a last look. When I had stood for some time on the eminence I thought of returning; and directing my steps toward Luachar, ascended a low hill in the neighbourhood, on the summit of which I took the foregoing description. I then went to the house, and after sitting a short time went out with the intention of going to the Rock of Ulladil - but I considered that night would fall before I would return, and so desisted.

I have acquired more just views of life, and am daily renouncing some of my sceptical opinions, and returning to my long abandoned common sense. I hope the time will yet come when I shall look with indifference upon the smiles and frowns of Fortune, and resign my thoughts into the hands of my Creator - when I shall consider all mankind as my brethren, look upon life with an indifferent eye, and upon death with the most serene resignation. At present I cannot help looking upon the vicissitutes of life with a kind of terror - Since I last left North Town, I have felt every day almost as long as a week at other times - this is not with me as with most others a symptom of lassitude; on the contrary it indicates enjoyment - When I have spent my time idly, or when nothing remarkable occurs, I look back upon days and weeks, nay, months, as the most insignificant portions of time. I never wish to kill time, hence the feeling of great length in it always affords pleasure - and I have this pleasure to add to the many enjoyments which I have experienced of late. If I had resolution, I should not despair.

Monday.
The weather was bad today with a strong southerly wind and rain. I rose before eight, and lay in wait for some ducks at which I fired without success.

I fired four shots through the day, without killing anything. About twelve I went to the ebb, where I gathered some shells; in this I was assisted by two little girls from Ceann-Resort - on returning I picked some pearls from the mussels gathered on Wednesday last - then began to learn to knit, under the tuition of Mrs MacDiarmid! In this employment I was occupied till teatime i.e. ten o'clock - I was so melancholy and impatient today, that I had almost determined to set off tomorrow for North Town - but I considered that this would be irresolution in the extreme; and so still continue resolved to visit the hills. I am afraid I shall not be able to reach Aberdeen in time for my Botanical Class - but I must not despair. I scrutinized the mill yesterday, and found the machinery exceedingly simple. The wheel which is very small is fixed to a perpendicular axis, the top of which is fixed in a piece of iron crossing the hole of the upper stone. This upper stone may be elevated or depressed by a contrivance similar to that used in the hand mill. Barley for broth may be made by steeping seed or grain for a few minutes in hot water, and then beating it in a bag, and the length of an hour only is required for the operation. It was the kind which we had to dinner today - It is very good - but not so agreeable as other barley - the food which we have used here is beef, goat-flesh, barley bread, potatoes, salmon, tea, milk, soup, butter, cheese - on this subject I am not so delicate as most - good wholesome food, prepared in the simplest way, is all that I require, or rather what I prefer - But were I more nice than I am, I might certainly be well pleased with my fare here. Sheep and goats, as well as cows eat sea-ware - the cattle here get their principal support from it in winter and spring.

Tuesday.

Today I slept till about ten - It had been nearly one before I went to bed last night, as I knew that I could not sleep - I have got such a habit of sitting up late, that I cannot get myself divested of it. Mrs MacDiarmid had the goodness to sit with me - After breakfasting, as the weather was pretty good, I went to Glen Ulladil, taking my gun and journal and the Pleasures of Hope with me. I sat down near the entrance of the glen to take a view. But as the lake was not in sight, I thought I should move a little farther up before taking a description. When I came within sight of the lake I observed two birds upon it, and upon getting near them found that there were three more. My gun refused fire several times - so I was obliged to leave them - they were of the same species as that which I killed at Ceanndibig. Ewen says that he has seen them in the sea, and that they do not pass the summer here. I intended to write a description, upon a small eminence near the lake; but on feeling for my ink bottle found that I had lost the pen. However memory will still enable me to describe this scene. Toward Luachar is a plain bounded on both sides by low hills - those on the south side more rocky than the others and having a considerable stream forming several small lakes running through it. Nearly in the middle of the valley rises a tremendous cliff, sloping rapidly and with a rounded outline on the south side, abrupt, and even declining from the perpendicular in some places, and retiring in others. The strata are perpendicular from the summit to the middle, where they become sloping & curvated or waving. The slope runs into the valley, and along it is a passage, very rugged and difficult, to a spot half way up the rock and at the base of the overhanging part, which was once the residence of a famous freebooter. Below this the base becomes broader and less abrupt and beneath the perpendicular part of the rock, debris consisting of immense masses, mingled with smaller fragments of rock are accumulated. Those nearest the rocks are smallest. The colour of the rock is dark blue, owing I believe to lichenous incrustation. This rock forms the extremity of a long ridge running from a very high hill at some distance, and removed from the sight. It is situated about the middle of the plain spoken of. To the south side of it a valley branches off from the main one on the plain, which I shall leave to pursue its own course among the hills - To the north side of the rock is the glen of Ulladil which passes more directly into the plain or great valley of which it appears to be the continuation or commencement. From the rock it is continued about half a mile, having on the south east side the rock of Ulladil continued along almost its whole course, but less majestic & much more broken than at the extremity, for a boundary - on the north west side the rugged and in some places nearly perpendicular declivity of a mountain, the highest part of which is seen in the distance, and crowns as it were the whole. The bottom of the glen is formed of two declivities coming from the rocks on either side, and at their union in the middle forming the bed of a stream which is seen falling wildly from the upper part of the glen. Among the rocks on the southern side is the cave. It is situated about the middle of the glen, and nearer the top than the bottom of the rocks forming the side or boundary. At this place are three ruts or furrows in the rock, of considerable size and nearly parallel. In the side of the one next this great rock is the cave, formed by a hollow left between strata of the rock. The more external part if artificial, being composed of a stone dyke or bulwark which closes up the space formerly constituting its mouth, and which extended along its whole length. Leaving the place from which I had this view (all excepting the cave and the fissures mentioned being seen from it) I went up the glen by the base of the rocks on the southern side till I came to the middle, when I ascended in the rut, and entered the cave. In doing which I experienced some difficulty as the stones were slippery with melting snow and ice, and the entrance to the cave is at the best very difficult, being such that one man might easily defend himself against a whole army. On entering the cave I found it very snug and warm; so I sat me down and read aloud a considerable portion of the Pleasures of Hope. The voice is heard here at least twice as loud and deep as in the open air. From over the wall which is in part fallen I had a fine view, of the mountain spoken of, of the upper part of the glen, and the rocks at hand, one of which juts out a great way opposite the cave. The floor of the cave is pretty plain toward the fore part, but farther back it inclines upward to meet the stratum forming the roof. In one end is a well. On leaving the cave I returned along the base of the cliffs, and ascended the Robber's stair for a considerable way. From the top of this I had an excellent view. The lake was just beneath me; and beyond it I could see the whole plain. I was overcanopied by the rock, which projected about fifteen feet beyond its base. I picked up some mineralogical specimens, and descending slowly and with difficulty, reached at length the border of the lake. Here I adjusted my portables, and proceeded homeward. Night fell before I was half way, and it now rained severely. So I did not get home till after seven - when I eat a good dinner, changed my stockings and trousers, and wrote this account. I have omitted to say anything of the lake, it is situated just under the rock, is of considerable size, very irregular in its outline and in other respects like the other lakes in the country. They have all the same character.

North Town, Friday, 27th February.

On Wednesday about eleven o'clock I left Luachar. Ewen and his wife accompanied me to the stepping stones on Amhin Shorsaidh, where we parted. I ascended Clar, and passed through the upper part of Glen Clar; then descended to Glen Langadil. I then ascended a short declivity and entered Gleann Bheagadil, through which I passed. Above Scaladil a very fine scene presented. To the northeast I had the Loch of Seaforth with its numerous windings; to the southwest a large valley bounded by dark cliffs on the north and southwest - The whole view terminated in Clisheim, and two peaks of less elevation. By the stream which runs through this glen I observed the roots of trees seven feet beneath the surface and a stump in a state of great preservation, the bark of which was about three feet beneath the present surface of the heath, indicating that a considerable quantity of soil has been heaped up since the period at which the trees grew. They were of the Scotch Fir species. I saw roots similar to these near Luachar by the side of Loch Resort, in a bank to appearance formed by the washing of the sea, and I am informed that others are found at Pabbay far under common low water mark. So that it would appear that the trees had grown before the sea occupied its present bed. This is not very improbable, as moss is well known to be an excellent antiseptic. No person capable of looking upon Nature without prejudice could view the Lochs of the Highlands and Isles without feeling a sort of conviction that they had been formed by the influx of the sea upon vallies. Loch Seaforth in particular cannot fail to enforce this idea, when one looks upon the mountains and vallies in its vicinity, and on its island, composed of a steep brown hill in every respect similar to the surrounding ones. I reached Marig in the dusk, where besides the family I saw Ioin mac Choinnich 'ic Ibher . The evening passed agreeably. The parson showed me a poem of his composition addressed to Mr Macleod of Harris, and asked my opinion of it. Although I thought little of it, I was in a manner compelled to say it was "very good". This answer betokens a woeful want of resolution, and shall not forgive myself for it. I told him however that it was incorrect in the number of syllables. This he denied - yet appeared afraid to subject it to scrutiny. There was a great deal of adulation in it - the part descriptive of the scenery of the country was very clumsily strained - The sentiments were rapid, and the versification harsh and most miserably defective. At each part which coincided with his ideas of elegance or wit, he punched my knees and hands most unmercifully. He has got into the notion that I intend to publish my journal, and so flatters at a prodigious rate. "When you descend the lofty summit of Clisheim", says he, "you will say at the foot of this mountain lives my friend Mr Macleod, in a lower tone adding, the parson of Harris!!! who has spent his time in solitude and contemplation!! Far from it Sir, thought I, keeping my mouth shut - Yesterday, I rose about ten - breakfasted - and about eleven left Marig, accompanied by Jane the minister's daughter and John McLeod. At Tarbert I saw the skin of a Swan - the plumage was white, the bill and feet duskyish, - 20 feathers in the tail. The bill like that of a goose. It was shot about Christmas last upon the lake above Urga. Jane was left in William Mackenzie's. We came over the hill of Luskentir with difficulty. The snow lay pretty deep in some places, and the wind was keen. John was reduced to the same condition to which I had been when going to Luachar. Near the summit we met a lad Nial Mac Thormoid 'ic Neil who gave each of us a bit of bread. On coming to Shelibost John applied for some meat, and got a large dish of oatmeal & hot water, named by the Lowlanders Brose, and by the Highlanders Pròis! Of this I partook, but was quickly obliged to desist, when the fellow, raking with his horn shovel, began to encroach upon the little spot which I had marked out for myself. I reached North town before eight. Mrs MacGillivray informed me that my uncle had been at Rodill where he saw the laird, who was very inquisitive about me, remarking that I was a very fine young man and amazingly clever: and pressed him to deliver his compliments and to tell that he should be very happy to see me at Rodill!!!!

Today I slept till near twelve. Little of importance was done. The shepherd has killed since I went away an Eagle, a Brent Goose and three ducks. The Eagle was kept for me - the following are the names of some hills, vallies, and streams near Luachar which Ewen had told me previous to my departure - and which I preserve partly because they may be of use in my poem, and partly because they are queer:

Dire Mor, Ullerabhal, Cneabare, Orabhal, Lag am foidhr, Gleann a Chlair, Gleann

Mhiabhag, Gleann Staoladil, Gleann h Usladir, Stron nan Leurd, Teinnisabhal, Caadal ghrannde, Caadal sfhiar, an Caisteal, an Ruidere, an Rapare, Cearascleid, Loch Thoisaruig, Loch an Fheoir, Loch Ulladil, Loch an fheoir, Loch a cheile, Loch bun an Fheircil, Amhin Shomharsaidh, Amhin mhor, Amhin Mhiabhag, Staolabhal, Stron ard, Loch Staoladil, Loch Lister.

Saturday.

Vultur Albiulla, Linnoi - White-tailed Eagle, Sea Eagle - An Iular riamhach-bhuidhe-ghlas- A fine specimen shot by the Shepherd upon the carcase of a horse.

This bird lives by rapine. Fish constitutes a principal part of its food. Hence it is often seen on the shores, and by the streams of this country. In the lambing season it plays great havock among the flocks but seldom carries off lambs unless from an eminence and when the wind is high. Ewen MacDiarmid says it sometimes kills the small sheep of the country breed, and that he has seen one attack a deer. It first mounted to a great height in the air, then darted down with amazing rapidity, fixed its talons in the shoulders of the deer, and struck it repeatedly with its wings about the eyes - When the deer fell the eagle again mounted to perform the same manoeuvre. If he had not risen from his place of concealment, he thinks the eagle would soon have mastered the deer. The other species found here, the Black Eagle is said to be more rapacious - Of this species I shot one some years ago - Linnous makes this which I have been describing a vulture, from there being no feathers between the eyes and bill - But there are thin bristly plumules - and as it agrees in every other aspect with the eagle kind, it should be referred to the genus Falco - it possibly forms the link between the two genera.

The weather is coarse today - so I am confined to the house. My Uncle intended to go to Rodill today, and I last night agreed to accompany him, but am now determined that I shall not. My pride could not stoop to such - the letter which I sent to the Inverness Journal about the Morse of Caolas Stocnis has appeared in my absence from home. The paper was sent to Mr Bethune in compliance with his request. I have again betaken myself to poetical composition - Last night I finished three stanzas of an address to the Harp of my Country, and have added one today - On Thursday I observed two ravens at Shelibost with straw in their bills. They have begun to nestle very early. The Snowdrop is in flower before now at Aberdeen; but here vegetation does not commence for many weeks yet, I must now think of leaving the country.

Wednesday, 4th March.

On Monday I went round the farm by the shore. Yesterday I scampered through Moll with my gun, and killed three Oyster-catchers, but they fell into the sea and drifted away. The birds which I saw on these two days were the Golden Plover, Oystercatcher, Great Black-backed Gull, Black-tailed Godwit, Turnstone, Lapwing, Shag, Skylark, Meadow Pipit, Stock Dove, Starling, Song Thrush, Raven, Hooded Crow, Curlew, Linnet, and Wren. Today I did not stir from home, but skinned the head and feet of the Eagle - I also dissected it in part. The whole body was thickly set with fine long down, which appeared without being mixed with feathers on the parts usually bare, viz a line on either side of the neck, one on each side under the wings, one along the centre of the sternum. My uncle has been at Rodill. Macleod (the Laird) again desired him to send me up.

Saturday 7th, March

My friends prevailed upon me to go to Rodill - on Thursday I rode to the Laird's. Leaving my horse at the stable, a low room of the old public house, I went to the great house! where I was kindly received by the Laird. On being conducted into the parlour I found Mr MacRae of Uist peripatizing there. So I got seated, drank a glass of wine, spoke to Mr McLeod upon sand & flowers. While dinner was putting upon table we walked to the Drawing Room where I was introduced to Mrs Macleod. Here the Laird and I played a long time at Battledoor. So, returning we dined, & drank about two bottles of wine - after which we again betook ourselves to the drawing room & drank coffee - After this, Toddy, and conversation till bed time. Mr MacRae and I slept together - The reverend gentleman assisted in a conversation of some hours length, in which the characters and accomplishments of certain Hebridean damsels held a distinguished part. He appears to think much of Marion MacCaskill, and not so much of Miss Shaw as to confirm the report I had heard. Yesterday we rose about eight. After breakfast Mr Macleod and I went to the churchyard where we planted some trees - the day was spent in walking up the Glen several times, in conversation, and reading. The evening passed as the last. The only additional incidents were Mrs Macleod playing several airs on the Piano-forte and Harp, & Miss Inglis's dancing. Mr & Mrs Macleod, and Master Finlay and I played at Battledore, i.e. I played with them all. After getting into bed we spent an hour or two in chatting as last night. Today we rose before eight, and went altogether to examine the Bishop's scholars. Oh! the fickleness of Fortune! Last year who was more in favour with the Laird than Armiger? Now he is not admitted to table - nor is the least regard shown toward him. After the examination he was invited to go and take a dram, which was given him in the lobby! So I may see that no friendship can last which is not founded on virtue. In the evening I left Rodill. Mr Mcleod wished "the pleasure of my company," as soon as I should find it convenient. On my way home I heard Throstles (Thrushes) singing in abundance. - This is the only fine day which we have had this fortnight.

Friday 13th, March

Little of importance has been done for some days. The laird accompanied by Messrs Stewart and MacRae were here on Wednesday. On some of these days I shot three Larks and a Starling, and my uncle two plovers. Today I have been employed in gathering some plants for Mrs Macleod. I find that I am still unreformed. My time is spent in apathy. I have promised tonight to set about a reformation immediately; and primo shall sketch a plan to regulate my conduct until I reach Aberdeen, when I shall probably possess better opportunities both of planning and practising. On glancing at the first chapter of my journal I find that some of the objects which I had in view while meditating my expedition have been shamefully neglected, and cannot be attained. Some however are still within my reach. On considering my present case, and taking a glance at some of my former plans, I find that the plans of the 10th January may suffice, together with that on a loose paper which I cannot at present refer to its proper place. All I have to add to these follows: I am to rise every day at dawn, to be in readiness to leave the country before tomorrow week. Before then 14 pages at least to be written - agriculture - economy to be described - every bird seen to be noted - a letter to my Uig girls - Mr MacG's and Mr Bethune's cases to be made up .

The shepherd tells me that the Black Eagle is much less than the brown, but is said to be more vicious. He has seen two attacking a deer in the same manner which Ewen MacDiarmid described. The vulgar firmly believe that the Eagle renews its age - but what idea they attach to the word renew I cannot gulp. However the shepherd says it casts its bill and claws, &c three times during its life, and this is renewal of age according to him. The period of its existence is great according to the following account. Trirduine fiodh, tri fiodh fidhach, tri fidhach iular, tri iular an domhan mhor - translated - the ages of three men equal that of a deer, of three deer, a raven; of three ravens an Eagle; of three eagles, the great world. So that if we take the life of a man to be 75, that of a deer is 225, of a raven 675, of an eagle 2025, and the duration of the world 6075 years. So according to this calculation we have 253 years till the end of time! He confirms Ewen's account of their killing sheep of the small breed; and adds that he has seen them take fish out of the sea.

Saturday 14th, March

Rose about seven, washed and cleaned myself, read a chapter of St. Mathew, then walked as far as the Chapel. On the way home I sketched the plan of my economical account of the country. On returning I wrote it as follows: The land is let to tennants of two descriptions, Tacksmen and Cotters. The Tacksmen possess individually large tracts of which they have leases. The cotters have either small portions individually, or large farms like those of the Tacksmen conjunctly. The first class commonly occupy their farms in part with their own stocking, and sublet the rest, usually a small portion, to cotters. Sometimes however the whole is sublet, and sometimes occupied exclusively by the Tacksmen. Among the small tennants the most general method is to take a farm conjunctly. Most of their farms thus form a kind of common wealth. The houses which are rude in structure and furniture are built together, but without order - their cattle are kept together while out of doors. The land under cultivation is not apportioned to each in his due quantity, but jointly occupied by all. Their mode is this. When a particular spot is to be turned, they divide it into small portions, and cast lots upon it - and thus the whole of the cultivated land is laid out. Among the common duties are herding the cattle, and guarding and watching the corn. These are performed either by persons hired for the purpose, or by one or two from each house in rotation. The cattle on the Tacksmen's farms are not housed in winter. Those on the cotter's commonly are. In summer the cows and milk sheep are sent to the glens, which are covered with heath and hard grass, sedges and rushes, because the part consisting of soft grass is not in general sufficient for their maintenance during the whole year. They are attended by a woman from each family, who has a small hut or shieling for her habitation, and who makes the cheese and butter. These however are made but in small quantity even on the best farm because the cows have very little milk, one that yields three pints a day besides the quantity necessary for the calf being considered a good milker. Some in fact can scarcely nourish their calves, and one calf sometimes requires the milk of two cows. This is rare however, and seldom practised, excepting in the case of rearing bulls. Black cattle are small, but very well shaped. They are covered with a thick and long pile to enable them to resist the winter's cold - a good pile is considered one of the best qualifications of a cow. The most common colours are black, brandered, brown or some of their colours mixed with white. These are standard colours. The sheep are of a small kind with white faces and legs and horned. The black faced breed has lately been introduced, and thrives well. Horses are kept in great numbers - They are small but robust, hardy, active, patient of labour, easily maintained, docile and peaceable. The pile of these is also thick and long - they are never shod. The farming utensils are coarsely manufactured by the inhabitants of the country - they will be described afterwards. The culinary ones are partly exotic, partly indigenous. Of the latter are cogs, spoons, ladle & c. The whole clothing excepting napkins and hats is manufactured in the country. That of the male consists of very thick and coarse woolen stuff, sometimes plain or of one colour, sometimes striped or crossed with a colour differing from the main one. This cloth is well adapted to the climate. From being thick and shaggy it resists the cold, and when wetted does not feel so uncomfortable as bare cloth. Short coats and wide trousers are commonly worn. The dress of the women consists of a gown composed of woolen cloth like the former but finer and bare and the other habiliments common among the same class in the lowlands - At other times it is a short wrapper and petticoat and this dress is by far the neatest, and indeed the best suited to the shape of the Hebridean damsels, who are in common short and 'robusteous'. Of this stuff the waistcoat of the male is made. The stockings are knitted as in the low country. The shoes are sometimes made of lowland leather, most commonly however of highland or half tanned. Hats and bonnets are worn; and of very late hats of sea bent (a grass) have been made in the country. Here are no dyers, candlemakers, butchers, tanners, and such - Every male who occupies land can knock a cow on the head, or cut the throat of a sheep, and steep his hides in Tormentic decoction: and every woman who assumes the office of a good wife, knows how to tinge her yarn, or dip a cotton rag in melted tallow. The only trades indispensable are those of the tailor, shoemaker, boat-carpenter, smith, and weaver. The professed shoemaker however is only necessary for when low country leather is used - for every tennant can make shoes of his own leather. The other trades are all exercised by the inhabitants in general, excepting those connected with imported articles, such as calico, iron, hemp, tobacco. The country does not yield all the articles necessary for subsistence. Iron and salt are only wanted however. The houses of the small tennantry are all built on the same plan. The wall is about six feet in height, composed of two facings of stone without clay or lime at the distance of about four feet from each other, and of earth which fills up the interval. The roof is of thatch, the couples & spars of oak and birch brought from the western shores of Ross and Inverness-shires. The apartments are commonly three: the first and largest occupies about one half of the house, and into it the door opens. The second occupies about a quarter, and the third the remainder. Nr 1 holds the cattle and lumber, Nr 2 is parlour, kitchen, dining room, nursery & c. Nr 3 Bedroom and granary. There are no chimneys, or even gables. The smoke fills the whole house, and vents partly by a hole about N.2, partly by the door, and some holes between the roof and wall formed as substitute for windows. The fire is placed in the middle of the floor in No 2, so that the members of the family may have the convenience of spreading their legs around it.

After breakfast I went by Moll with my gun as far as Amhin Laidhnis where I pulled some plants of Honeysuckle and Hypericium for Mrs MacLeod. On returning I found Mrs Campbell from Scarista in the house. In compliance with her request Mrs MacG. had prepared some tea, of which I partook. Till evening I was occupied in writing various articles. At dinner Mrs MacG. was affected with a slight hysterical paroxysm, and continued some what indisposed through the night. She cut my hair in the evening however - After this I noted the following particulars concerning agriculture:

The whole country may be laid out into two general divisions, one comprehending all the interior composed of hills and vales and plain covered with heath excepting where the bare rock projects through the soil, which at this moment reminds one of a poor man's skin appearing through his rags; the other composed of that portion of land which skirts the shores. This varies in breadth and is by no means continuous. In fact it is only so on part of the west coast. Its soil is various: on the tract mentioned principally sandy, in most other places half-reclaimed moss, at Rodill an excellent black or dark brown mould. In quantity too it is equally varying - The subsoil is generally gravel or clay. The solid rock appears here and there forming great inequalities, so that in the whole country there is not a plain half a mile square. Large fragments of rock also frequently lie upon the surface. This is the portion appropriated to culture, and is separated from the others by stone or turf dykes. The shores in most places produce abundance of seaweeds - and upon the sands vast quantities are thrown up in winter. The labours of the husbandman commence about the beginning of February, when he begins to cut the sea ware and to spread it upon the ground. This together with what he may have found during the winter, he covers with turf and earth, forming long ridges about five feet in breadth, and of indefinite length, separated by a chasm varying in size, from which the soil covering the seaware has been taken. These ridges always run along a declivity so as to allow the water to escape without doing damage. They are seldom straight owing to the irregularity of the ground. At this work he is generally employed for about two months, or at least six weeks. At the end of which time he turns the land which had been manured last year, and takes in new. The instruments employed are - for the first, the cas dìrach, something like a spade, but very clumsy, and without the cross handle. Its action is nearly that of the spade; but it requires two people, one to work it, the other to throw the turf upon the ridge; for the second the cas chrom which turns the mould like the plow, and is well adapted for thin soil. In the first potatoes or barley are planted; in the second Barley and oats according to its nature. The last seed is sown about the twentieth of May. The cattle are allowed to trample upon the corn land, and even to crop the blade for some weeks after it appears, partly from inactivity, and partly from the want of fences. The plough is only used by some few Tacksmen. In most places it cannot be used from the irregularity of the ground. On ground manured with seaweeds, potatoes or barley are sown - Next year oats will be raised. Dung yields three crops; potatoes, barley, oats, in succession. The rotation in tolerable soil is this: first year, oats: dung being then laid on, next year potatoes; next barley; then oats, sometimes two crops. It is then allowed to run, into grass, in which condition it remains for three or four years. Potatoes make the principal part of the crop, and upon them the poor people chiefly subsist. They are in general bad, being very watery. This is probably owing to the want of change in seed: it being a well-known fact, that the natives of warm climates degenerate in cold. In strong land an instrument like the cutter of a plough is used to cut the roots preparative to the action of the cas chrom. No carts are used, and indeed could not from the nature of the surface. Sea ware and dung are carried in creels on the backs either of men or of horses. Turnips have only been tried on two farms, Ensay and North Town they appear to agree wonderfully with the climate. The climate is damp and boisterous. From October to

April almost continual rains, snow at times, westerly and northerly winds, with tremendous storms. From that to the middle of May dry weather with easterly winds. The summer is often cold and generally wet: but August and September are commonly mild and clear.

Tacksmen might live very comfortably were they industrious enough but they are in general too idle and too prejudiced to mend their mode of living. The sea in all places abounds in fish; the heaths and fields and shores with wild fowls of various kinds - The fields might produce potatoes, barley, and oats in sufficient quantity: the hills beef and mutton. But as matters stand at present, both rich and poor tennants live rather miserably, particularly the latter. The country is evidently overstocked with inhabitants, and must continue to be more so every day; because it is not capable of improvement equal to the increase of inhabitants.

In regard to Botany, North town alone would be an excellent school for two years. To more than this the country can have no pretensions. In the evening as Uncle Toby and I were playing at drafts, a tremendous - pshaw! nothing of consequence - only remember poor Peggy, the daughter of Tormid bàn, from Toray.

North Town, Sunday.

It was nine before I got up today. In the morning I went to South Town - The weather was rainy, but not very cold. On Tashtir I saw a small flock of Snow-buntings. Larks were singing today. After breakfast I spoke to my uncle about his wife's complaint, advising him to send a man to Inverness for the medicine requisite. To this he did not assent. After twelve I took a solitary walk to Boter where I enjoyed the pleasure of agitating several things of importance. Among others I determined the folly and impropriety of entertaining any hatred to Miss MacDonald, and Donald Stewart, to the former for having injured me in traducing my character, to the latter, because I conceive him to be a very bad man. I felt the serenity which a consciousness of being at peace with oneself and with all mankind affords. After walking upwards of an hour I returned. I had intended to write Mrs Mac's case today, but she wishes to put it off for the present - so I must yield.

Wednesday   March.

On Monday the weather was most delightfully serene till after twelve. At night it blew a perfect hurricane from the west. Westerly winds are the most boisterous. In the forenoon I went to Rodill, taking with me a boy to carry plants for Mr Macleod. At Creag bheist I added some specimens to my stock. At Rodill I meet the Laird with Mrs Macleod and Miss Harriet walking. So in due time we entered the house. At dinner and through the evening we talked on Botany, Poetry &c. Mr Macleod had been told I was a poet (probably by Mr MacRae) I owned I had scribbled a little - So he pressed me to recite some pieces, which I did. He thought them "very fine", that is, he said so, and desired me to leave a copy of one to which I assented. Mrs Macleod played on the Piano. After she retired we sat sometime drinking toddy. I received a letter today from Mr Craigie, which afforded me a prodigious deal of pleasure. On retiring to my bedchamber I read it again with great delight. I did not sleep till about two, with thinking on various subjects, particularly Aberdonian scenes. On Tuesday the weather was bad. After breakfast I read a little, and before dinner took a pretty long walk with Mr Macleod. The evening was spent as usual. Mr Macleod played on the Harp. When here, I am almost constantly tipsey - Primo before breakfast a glass of aqua vita, which taken into an empty stomach makes one's head reel. 2nd a glass of wine at noon, which keeps up in a faint degree the effect of the former, 3rd A glass at dinner, and after it about half a score, 4th Toddy after nine o'clock till bed time. In fact I think all this is just not very proper, but there is no denying Mr Macleod, he is so very pressing - Today I got up about six, and left Rodill, after having promised to go down tomorrow before ten to stuff the Bear, which is about to be killed. I arrived at North Town before nine - The good people there were still in bed - So I told them the news I had to communicate regarding the farm, observing conclusorily that they had no occasion to lament the dearness of the place when they considered how industrious they were. This of course ironically. After breakfasting, I rode to Borve, where I chatted a long time, drew the first sketch of the Minister's case, dined, & c. In the evening I returned. My papers came from Pabbay last Monday so I fall to transcribe some particulars regarding birds and quadrupeds, which are noted among them: and just those which are most perfect.

Sturnus vulgaris Starling Truid
Nidification. Their nests are composed of grass, feathers, hair, loosely put together. Eggs ovate elliptical, pale blue - 4-6, very large. May and June.

Food - Worms & insects which they pick commonly from among cow's dung. In Harris they are seen attending the herds in large flocks, often perching on the backs of Black-cattle, horses, and sheep. As this bird is gregarious it is worth shooting - six or ten might often be killed at a shot. The Harrisian sportsmen decapitate them, as they have a notion that poison is contained in the head. It is a garrulous bird, and may be taught to imitate the human voice.

Columba Oenas - Rock Pigeon - Stockdove - Calman

Habitation - Caverns of the Hebrides along with the Starling and Shag. Immense numbers are found among the rocks of Ben Capval and of Pabbay Island in Harris. Numerous also in Uig in Lewes - seen at Luachar.

Nidification - Nuptials are celebrated with much cooing and circumambulation on the part of the male. Monogamy - Nests are composed of grass, carelessly patched up. Eggs two, white, ovate, elliptical, several broods are produced during the Summer and Autumn. They commence as early as March.

This being a gregarious bird is an excellent subject for the sportsman. I have heard of eighteen being killed at one shot. I have killed nine. They collect in large flocks in winter, feeding on the stubble lands. In summer when grain cannot be obtained they pick the small animals found among the grass. In winter, if the snow lies long upon the ground, they frequent the cornyard.

This is undoubtedly the original of the House pigeon - I have seen tame pigeons mingling with the wild ones, and wild pigeons brought from the rocks when young, have been tamed, and have paired with domestic ones.

Turdus musicus - Throstle - Mavis - Smeorach. (Song Thrush)

Habitation - In Harris, where there is a wood, sides of hills, and vallies. In winter frequents cornyards, and is seen about houses. In some places they frequent the shores in great numbers, feeding upon the whelk. Monogamous - not gregarious-

Nidification. Nest composed of heath, straw, lined with mud - very compact - Eggs about 4, bluish with a few red spots-

Food - vermin and insects, particularly the Lumbricus terestris. (Earthworm) In its wild state its song has an exquisitely melancholy effect in the summer evenings among the solitary glens of the Hebrides.

This bird is not inelegant. The breast is beautifully coloured. In winter they are found about houses and cornyards in considerable numbers.

Tringa nigricans - Purple Sandpiper.

Food - small testacea picked up along the shore. This is one of the tamest birds with which I am acquainted, allowing a person to approach within five or even four paces - Mr Norman MacNiel says he has seen them killed with a tangle. It does not appear that they are numerous here. I have seen them at North Town, Ensay, and Pabbay; at times in flocks, at times one by one. They pick up their food quite close to the wave. Hence while searching they are in continual motion, running out as the wave retires, and retreating as it advances. I have never seen them on land.

Thursday Evening, Rodill - Bedroom in the house of my friend the Squire of Harris, half past ten, a rainy night. Today the weather has, as usual, been coarse. I rose about half eight, breakfasted and equipped me for a journey to this place where I arrived after ten. I found the laird by the parlour fire reading as is his custom when he cannot get out to walk. So "your servant Sir", and "how are you today?" and very well Mrs Mac, I'm glad to see you, sit down - and so on. So I began to read some of Forte's comedies and so on till about two when I was desired to go to the drawing room, when I saw Mrs Mac, Miss Harriet, and Degraves's children, & took a glass of wine - The day passed as usual. The death of Master Bruin is to be deferred till tomorrow morning at six o'clock.

Mrs Macleod is a young lady of about seventeen, highly polished in mind and body: perfectly free from pride, and apparently from conceit. In her person she is elegant, in her demeanour courteous, in action graceful - in short a most accomplished woman. Her face, neck, shoulders and breast are most elegantly moulded, but she is rather slender. In fact she has the thinnest arms, and legs I have seen - but she is a child I may say and will no doubt mend. She does not talk pertinaciously, or even with assurance. Her part is not proud, nor her manner authoritative - that is, whether from youth, or natural inclination, or prior circumstances, or all three, she has more of the mildness, modesty, condescension goodness of a well concated but poor girl, cast in the finest mould of nature, than either of an advocate's daughter, or a squire's lady.

North Town, Friday, 20th March.

Rose today about six. The ground was covered with snow. I found a musket, and charged it with powder in due quantity and a lump of lead. So poor Bruin was shot through the head. After breakfast I skinned him, and before dinner made up a body of sticks and hay for him - and that was all. In consequence of having heard some disagreeable news regarding my uncle I left Rodill after drinking coffee, about seven o'clock - the moon shone now and then - large showers of snow so I got home in good trim - and what about it.

Saturday.

Went to Rodill today - where I dined. I found that I had taken a wrong method in stuffing the bear, and so determined to have him taken up here, which is to be done on Monday. On my way down I meet Master Lachlan going to Scarista, where he is to preach tomorrow. In the evening I returned. I was wetted to the skin.

Now Sir, I have got to the end of another week; and am upon the whole not ill pleased with my performance. If I mend as much next week, why - I shall be tolerable. So let one fall to it then - But, I'll have no restrictions, i.e. none imposed by myself. Yet I think that to exercise my resolution I shall abstain from smoking Tobacco, and shall rise every morning at six o'clock.

Now for the transcription of my papers from Pabbay.

Anas Cygnus. Swan. An Eala.

On their passage southward they frequently sit on the lakes of Uist, and sometimes on those of Harris. Master Lachlan says he has seen them at St Kilda.

Anas Anser. Great Lag. Wild Goose. Giadh glas.

Breed in the island in the sound of Harris. In Harvest they often destroy much barley - are seen here all winter. Localities - Islands near Ensay, Loch-na-Morchadh, Northtown, Little Borve. They are said to be exceedingly numerous in Uist.

Anas Boschas. Mallard

Breed in marshy grounds, and by the sides of lakes. Feed by night. In winter frequent the marshy grounds at Scarista and Ui in pairs. Not numerous here.

Scolopax Arquata. Curlew. Guilbhnach.

Are found every where by the sea shore - very numerous upon Ui. Excellent eating - but very shy, they frequent the shores and low grounds in large flocks, and are so careful as not to allow a nearer visible approach than 300 yards or more.

Charadrius pluvialis. Green Plover. Feadag.

While breeding they remain in the heaths. In Autumn they collect into large flocks, remaining still in the hills. In winter, especially during frost they descend to the coast, and at low water are seen picking their food along the shores. Cow dung on the heath is often seen riddled by the thrusting in of their bills in search of food. They are said to be fattest in spring. When in flocks they are easily approached; and at all times more so than most birds. They are particularly tame while nesting so as to allow a person to approach so near as ten or even seven yards - At this time the heaths resound with their cries.

Alauda pratensis - Titlark. Glaip-ian. Meadow Pipit

Frequents the sea shore for the insects found among the weeds. Nest by a turf, or in a sheltered place among rushes. Eggs 4.

Homatopus Ostralegus. Oystercatcher

Habitation - rocky shores. Food shellfish, particularly the limpit it is said, to the separating of which from the rocks the bill is peculiarly well adapted. Gregarious for the greater part of the year. When in flocks are so shy that they are approached with almost as much difficulty as the curlew. The flesh is tough.

Tetras lagopus - Ptarmigan - An Tàrmagan.

Habitation - summits of the highest hills, at Ronaval, and Benluskentir. It allows a person to approach within twelve or even six paces, and crouches when a stone is thrown over its head. They have been killed with sticks. Its voice is a sort of croak.

Pelecanus Bassanus. (Gannet)

Habitation. Rocks of Hirt, in immense numbers. Nest composed of grass. One egg, larger than a Turkey's. White. April and May. They are killed by the inhabitants for the sake of their feathers and under night. One man is able to kill seven hundred in a night. In each large flock a sentinel remains awake, which the bird killer contrives to silence first. He then tickles the rump of the nearest, which falls a singing, or chattering, without however raising its head from its wing. His next neighbour follows his example and so on till the whole join in chorus. Amid this general chatter, which is no doubt meant as a mutual assurance of safety, the murderer finds it an easy matter to run over the whole, as he merely squeezes the body between his knee to prevent flapping of the wings, & bends the neck suddenly backward which is sufficient to kill them. They disappear about the beginning of November, and return in March - such is Master Lachlan's account; and I believe, Mr McNiel of Pabbay who was Tacksman of Hirt for many years, confirms the statement. The birds are thrown down from the cliffs next morning & picked up by a boat which comes for that purpose.

It is to be seen through the summer and autumn flying along the shores of Harris. On seeing its prey, it dashes headlong into the water, often disappearing for the space of a minute. On emerging it sits upon the water for a short time, and then rises to pursue its employment. It is almost as incessantly on the wing as the swallow, nor have I ever seen or heard of an instance of its being found sitting on shore. Sometimes they are found so full as to be unable to rise. When a boat approaches them while in this state they disgorge the contents of their stomachs with great rapidity according to Mr McNiel of Pabbay. Their most common rout is along the shores; and in their course though a peninsula should occur they seldom cross by the land, but almost constantly follow every sinuosity of the shore. I have however seen them crossing from Bunanoish to Traigh-na-clibhe; and I remember to have got one near the house, some years ago, which was knocked down by an eagle. In summer there is an annual mortality among them. At this season they are found dead on the shores, and on the sea. For the first year it is, like young gulls of a greyish colour.

Pelecanus Graculus. Scart. Scarbh. (Shag)

Habitation. Maritime cover of the Hebrides, to which they resort in immense numbers. In the morning they may be seen at South town covering the sea to a considerable extent, on their passage from the caves of Liuir and so to their fishing stations in the sound of Harris. I have counted 105 in one flock, and the number exceeded this very considerably, as many were under water at the time - the nest is composed of seaweeds, heather and other materials picked up on the water, clumsily put together. Eggs two or three, bluish white, sub-elliptical, very narrow in proportion to their length. May, June. The young are covered some weeks with a black down - While commencing the act of diving they rise with a spring entirely out of the water. Though a very coarse and indelicate bird, they are eaten by the poor people here. The young are very delicate, and previous to being full fledged have not the fishy taste of the full grown ones. monogamous.

Corvus Corax. Raven. Fighach. Biodhdach.

Habitation - High rocks, especially those impending the sea. Food of every kind, poultry, eggs, grain & c. Nest is built in the inaccessible part of rocks, of sticks, seaweeds, hair, wool, straw. Eggs 4 to 6 - March and April. In harvest they become sub-gregarious, when they make great havock in some places among the barley. At other times, they are commonly seen in pairs; excepting for some weeks after bringing their brood abroad when the whole family adheres. I have seen one with a good deal of white in its plumage. It was reckoned the harbinger of some calamity!

Rallus Crex. Land Rail. Corncrake. An Dreanne.

Habitation, Corn fields, long grass; commonly found in Harris among the Yellow Iris. Nest of grass, on the ground. Eggs 6-10 - oval, whitish with red spots. The young forsake the nest immediately after exclusion, and are covered with black down. It is very delicate eating, & upon their first arrival here might be found in considerable numbers, as the grass is then very short. I have caught them alive. They arrive about the middle of May, and disappear about the end of July, at least become mute at that time - Its note is crex repeated.

Rallus aquaticus. Water Rail.

Habitation unknown to me. My uncle saw one while we were at Luachar by Amhin Resort. As it flew badly, he pursued it, but soon lost sight of it. I saw one since in Allt-an-Liuir at North town, but it concealed itself among the banks. The shepherd says he saw one in the same place, two years ago - as in the foregoing, the body is very much compressed.

Scolopax Gallingo - Snipe. Nàosg.

Habitation, marshes, moors, margins of lakes. Found in winter nights in great numbers on Ui and the low grounds of Scarista. Nest on the ground, composed of grass. Eggs 3. Ovato-conical. In summer they fly to a great height, making at times a noise resembling thunder, or perhaps the bleating of a goat (hence their name of Gobhar aidhir, air goat,) at which time they flap their wings very quickly.

Sunday.

The weather was bad today. I did not rise till after eight. After breakfast I read some of the Bible; and wrote some of the above. Before dinner I walked to near Buninos solus, and after it to Ui with Mrs MacGillivray. I have read the book of Job, and Solomon's song, and would think the first to have been written without inspiration, and the other to have no spiritual meaning. Of course I may be mistaken. I like the book of Job very much as I have already said.

List of Birds found in Harris with their localities

For the sake of arrangement I shall associate each species with the part in which it is usually found. Land and Sea obviously form the two primary divisions. The latter admits of only two subdivisions: the open sea, and that along the coast. The former I divide into Fields, Hills and shores - the division Lakes & Rivers is an adjunct to the two former - that of cornyard to the first. The department Fields includes the varieties of ground usually found within dykes, which may be divided into dry & wet. That of Hills includes all without dykes consisting of hills and vallies covered with earth, and divisible into dry and wet as the former. The shores are rocky and sandy.

	Land.
Fields, dry.	Skylark, Meadow Pipit, Linnet, Stock Dove, Corn Bunting, Song Thrush, Starling, Curlew, Raven, Hooded Crow, Wren, Blackbird, Reed Bunting, Common Gull, Golden Plover, Grey-lag Goose, Swan, Hedge Sparrow, Whimbrel, Sand Martin, Corncrake, Pied Wagtail, Yellow Wagtail, Stonechat, Fieldfare, Redwing.
wet.	Snipe, Mallard, Water Rail, Lapwing, Woodcock.
Hills, dry.	Red Grouse, Golden Plover, Raven, Ptarmigan, Great Black-backed Gull, Song Thrush, Blackbird, Hedge Sparrow, Reed Bunting, Sea Eagle.
wet.	Snipe, Water Rail, Mallard, Woodcock.
Shores. rocky.	Common Gull, Greater Black-backed Gull, Curlew, Oystercatcher, Blacktailed Godwit, Golden Plover, Song thrush, Meadow Pipit, Turnstone, Heron, Hooded Crow, Sea Eagle.

sandy.	Common Gull, Greater Black-backed Gull, Curlew, Blacktailed Godwit, Golden Plover, Ringed Plover, Turnstone, Sea eagle, Common Tern, Snow Bunting.
Rivers.	Dipper, Water Rail.
Lakes.	Mallard, Grey-lag Goose, Swan, Coot, Moorhen.
Cornyard & about houses	Linnet, Corn Bunting, Skylark, Starling, Reed Bunting, Song Thrush, Hedge Sparrow, Wren.

	Sea.
By the shore.	Shag, Cormorant, Eider Duck, Goosander.
Open Sea.	Storm Petrel, Fulmar.

Tuesday.

I have done little today. Mr John MacDonald from Rodill came here today. In the evening my uncle arrived from Luskentir along with Mr Murdoch MacLellan of Scalpay. I have written a little today preparatively to my departure.

Thursday.

Yesterday morning my uncle and Murdoch and Sir John Stobbie went to Rodill. I was occupied all day in stuffing the bear. In the afternoon Mrs Mac received letters from her sisters, with compliments of course for me. Nelly gave an account of their sorrow at parting with me I don't know how - but I have loved the whole of this family since my first acquaintance with them. In the evening I was told by Isabeil ni' Challum 'ic Ailein that there was a man at the end of the house wishing to speak with my aunt Mrs Mackay. So I went out to find him. Co th'ann? said I. No answer. Is it you who want Mrs Mackay? Oh! how are you Mr MacGillivray? exclaimed poor Angus Mackay. He had come from Glasgow with his three children, driven away by the cruelty of the creditors.

Today I finished the stuffing of the bear. The plan which I took was this - First I got a frame made to support the stuffing. It consisted of a stick for the back, two cross ones to which were affixed those substituted for the bones of the legs, and a neck piece, upon these straw and hay were moulded into the natural form of the animal, and the whole secured by ropes. I then sewed up the skin, and slit it from the tail to the head along the back - and thus the skin was easily drawn upon the legs, and from thence pulled over the whole body - The head was supported by a rope. In the evening I put him out, and was amused with the apprehension with which the dogs and some little boys regarded him. My uncle has not yet returned.

Friday.

Rose at half past six, and set out for Rodill, where I arrived before breakfast time. I found my uncle in Donald MacDonald's. Mr MacLellan took us to John Macleod's to get our morning. Murdoch, Duncan his brother, John McLeod, my uncle and I composed the party. We drank a mutchkin. We breakfasted in John MacDonald's. The company exclusive of those mentioned were Rory MacNiel of Caolas Uist, Donald MacDonald, Mrs MacDonald and John MacDonald. After this Uncle Toby and I steered for North town where we arrived about twelve. My intention in going to Rodill was merely to speak to my uncle about Angus - so we talked about him and his family by the way. At Donald Ross's we drank half a mutchkin, with the assistance of the good man and Conish mac Ioin 'ic Dhomhnuill. I saw the Coltsfoot in flower near the houses of North Town.

Omissions - Saw a Rook some days ago near the house, the only one seen here this winter - a proof of the comparative mildness of the season, for in very severe ones they appear in large flocks. Lapwings are seen in Moll. The Lark and Throstle sing always when the weather is fine. A good way of pleating the ruffles of skirts is to crimp a little, & then leave a small space plain, repeated ad limitem!

Gaelic Names of Birds

An Iular	Hawk	An Uiseag	Skylark
An Iular	Hawk	Glas-ian	Meadow Pipit
An Seothag	Hawk	Naosg }	Snipe
An Smeorach	Song Thrush	an Gobhar aidhir}	
Truid	Starling	An Calman	Stock Dove
A Chuag	Cuckoo		

An Siollt	Goosander	An Trilleachan	Oystercatcher
An Lach	Mallard	Am Feadag	Ringed Plover
Am Faoileag }	Common Gull	Am bicoin	Linnet
An Scaireag }		An dreathan	Wren
Am Farspag-ach	Great Black-back	A Mhallag	Sand Martin
An Turo bhuachaill		An Gochan Uisg	Dipper
An Scarbh	Shag	An Lon Dubh	Blackbird
Scarbh uchd-gil	Cormorant	A Ghuilbnach	Curlew
Scarbh buill		An Eala	Swan
Stearnein-ag	Swallow	Am Biodhtach	Raven
Sulear	Gannet	An Fheannag }	Hooded Crow
An Coileach }	Red Grouse	Starrag }	
		Breachd-an-t-sil	Pied Wagtail
Am Fudagag }	Woodcock	An Clacharan	Stonechat
An Coileach Coille }			
An Tarmachan	Ptarmigan	A Churuchdag	Lapwing
An Dreanne	Corncrake	A Bhothag	Ringed Plover
An Craidh			
-ghiadh	Sheld Duck		

Phoca vitulina - Seal - Ron

The specimen - a young one, probably about six months old, and not exceeding 3 feet from the snout to the end of the tail - a male.

In this individual the process of depilation was going on - the old pile was whitish, the new which was perfect only about the neck was of a beautiful light blue mixed with grey, very short and thickly set. It was killed by the shepherd, at Buninosh, with his stick, having been found ashore at low water. Tongue fleshy, flat, rounded at the extremity, imarginate - bifid.

Dissection. Under the skin was an universal layer of fat or blubber, about an inch and half in thickness. The liver was very large, divided into many lobes with a gall-bladder. The intestines very small. Eyes orbicular - pupil dark-green. The central part of the retina being of a most beautiful blue, tinged with green.

Food - fish

Manners. They are seen in the water, seldom in any considerable number together, appearing above the shoulders, very often following boats or along the shores. They come ashore to bring forth (give birth), and often doze upon the rocks at low-water, or rather, it is said, at half tide. When ashore they do not walk but with difficulty and are easily overtaken - a blow on the nose is said to kill them instantly, while their skull is so hard that one might pelt at it for an hour with little effect.

Locality - Among the islands in the sound of Harris very frequent. The rock of Gaskir, 12 miles from Harris in the Atlantic is a great place of resort. Great numbers are killed here annually. Upwards of a hundred and twenty have been killed in one season and in one day. In the latter end of Autumn or beginning of Winter a boat goes from the Island of Taransay near the mainland, when the seals are found in shore. The men armed with cudgells wait in a narrow passage for their approach, and by dexterously hitting the nose kill the greater part of the herd. Some of immense size are sometimes found, said to be as large as a cow. Of such the skins and blubber are embarked, those of a small size are carried home entire. The island of Haskir in Uist, similarly situated is alike famous as being the resort of these animals.

The flesh is sometimes eaten by the poor people - The skin forms an excellent covering for Trunks.

Cervus Elaphus - Red Deer - Fiadh - Tamh Gridhach, Laogh.

Numerous in the plains of Harris and the heath of Lewes - more especially in the latter district, though not so much so now as formerly. They were about twenty years ago so plentiful that the poor people had much ado to keep them from their corn which they came to eat under night, and the lairds were so barbarous as to prohibit the use of guns. Since Local Militia however has been raised they have very rapidly decreased owing to the number of muskets introduced by that institution.

The male alone carries horns, which are incurvated and branched. The number of branches on each horn has been found in this country amounting to eleven or twelve. Eight however is considered as the highest in the ordinary run. They are said to shed their horns annually and I have seen some in a shepherd's house at Loch Carron of a very large size which were found in the hills there. The chief peculiarity about the head is a deep oval pit under the nasal angle of the eye containing a substance resembling - cerumen (earwax). The back and sides are reddish brown, the belly & perineum dirty white. The female is much less robust than the male. Both have a bump on the forehead. They feed through the night, and rest for a great part of the day - the rattling (rutting) season is from Michaelmas till Martinmas when the stags bellow, roll themselves in mud and pools, and undergo so much fatigue as to become very lean. The females increase in weight till Christmas. It is a very vigilant and timid animal - approached with great difficulty. It requires considerable knowledge to enable one to become an expert huntsman. Care must be always taken to keep upwind as their sense of smelling is very acute. They are usually killed with with swan or buck shot, sometimes with ball. Five have been killed with one shot. One man has killed eighteen in a season.

Sunday, 29th March, 1818.

Yesterday Norman MacDonald, Messenger from Uist was here about my uncle's affairs. In the evening Mr Stewart came from Rodill. I am detained from setting out some days by my uncle. His lease is out at Whitsunday, and he is not sure of getting his present farm again - The weather was wet but not very cold today. I walked as far as the chapel of South town from which I saw two Solan Geese coasting. The sight of these afforded me much pleasure - but it gave pain also when I reflected that the season was far advanced and I still here.

In regard to my behaviour last week. I may say I have done well. I am certainly improving. I want to acquire determination, to enable me to break off vicious habits, and to be in readiness for any enterprise of importance that may be suggested by circumstances - and the best plan for acquiring the resolution I conceive to be to impose now and then little tasks upon myself. All the faculties of the mind are improved by exercising them. To this work I have already begun: for I have given up the habits of smoking and snuffing which I had acquired - habits which if not absolutely vicious, were yet disgusting to some and prejudicial to myself. These I do not mean to relinquish entirely: for I shall still allow myself the liberty of taking a whiff or a pinch upon occasion. It is only the habit that I militate against - and this I shall assuredly break off for the present at least. In my attempts to break off some of the habits I have not succeeded: for instance that of sleeping too long in the morning and that of being peevish at times. On the other hand, however, I have gained much, I have learned to detest lying and swearing and profanity of every kind - so that a strict adherence to truth and decency of behaviour shall in future be principal traits in my character. I find that when I impose too many resolutions at once, I am bewildered as it were among them: and that I succeed better when I confine my efforts to a few points. So far this week I shall only continue my efforts to acquire the habit of early rising - at the same time I must not lose what I have already gained.

Friday, 3rd April.

For three days past the weather has been delightfully serene. On Tuesday I went to Borve. At Scarista on my way I entered the schoolhouse where I saw the Bethune children. The deputy schoolmaster and William went to show me a Raven's nest. It was composed of heather, twigs of willow, & the roots of the Sea Bent and Lady's Bedstraw. At Borve I was introduced to Mr Grant of Ulinish in Skye and his daughter: the former a good looking pleasantish, sensible gentleman, the latter tolerably well formed, but without anything interesting in her appearance, or manner. As I was returning in the evening I met John MacDonald of Scarista who had got some news from Uist relative to my Uncle - this he deferred to a future opportunity. On Wednesday I shot two pigeons. My uncle went to Uist. Yester morning I went to see John MacDonald but did not find him. I then crossed the hill above Scarista and traversed the moor till I came into the road near the Mill. In this course I shot three plovers, which were very fat, and had a black spot on the breast and belly. I arrived at Rodill about half past three. My object in going there was to show Mr MacLeod some papers relative to the distribution of my father's* effects. This I did. Here I found Mrs Campbell of Keligray, with Miss MacNiel and Mr Cameron. The latter is Teacher to Mrs Campbell's children, and had just arrived from Aberdeen where he had been making a partial session at the Divinity Hall. He had no news of importance for me; but that Mr Mackie had advertised a course of Lectures on Botany, and that some of my friends had been inquisitive about me. After dinner I scampered home. On the way I shot a goose upon Loch-an-fheoir but did not kill. I arrived about eight o'clock somewhat fatigued. In the glen above Ob the snipes and throstles were occupied in editing their respective notes. The whole glen was in an uproar with them. The snipe was also thundering on wing. Gannets are now seen daily on the coast. I have seen the Stonechat today, for the first time this season. I am obliged to wait till the Set, (the meeting with the laird and his Factor to set the tenancy and rent) which takes place about the end of next week as I may be of assistance to my uncle.

* This, and a later one in this journal, is the only reference to his father that MacGillivray makes in any of his published work, or in any of his letters that I have seen.

Wednesday.

For about seven days we have had easterly winds - they continue. A good deal of snow has fallen since Sunday. Yesterday I saw a flock of Snow Buntings. Stonechats are common. Today I went to Borve, though the weather was extremely cold. Here I dined and drank tea. Before dinner Mr Macleod of Marig with his son James came. Between dinner and tea time I was employed in reciting poetry to Misses Bethune and Grant. They prevailed upon me to promise to write some of my own verses for them. This evening passed most agreeably. I was in good glee, and had the satisfaction of seeing myself looked upon as the greatest personage among the strangers!!! I have got even familiar with Miss Jessy Grant, and am just prepared to - Did I say so - Remember - Yes my dear — you are ever ever present. I would not give up your place in my heart to - the Queen of Sheba. About half past eight I left Borve, and got home before ten. The weather was very bad, and the sand wet - and so I got a headache by the way. I have learned part of the manual exercise from Angus Mackay, and perhaps attained that dexterity in the use of the gun which had been a desideratum.

Friday 10th, April

Yesterday my uncle and I went to Rodill, the Set having commenced. Mr Macleod with his Factor Donald Stewart* were seated at a large table giving audience. Soon after our entering the room my Uncle was asked if he had anything to say. He replied that he was desirous of settling "It is needless," said Macleod hastily, "to be talking of North Town: it is already set! Are you inclined to bid for any other farm?" My uncle answered in the negative. In the course of a conversation on the subject the Laird was reminded of his promises, but he did not in sooth regard promises that had been made last year. So my uncle was silenced. But I who had not till now opened my lips, could no longer restrain my indignation against that spirit which

*Donald Stewart had the farm of Luskentyre as a sheep-farm, and was also factor of the Harris estate. He used this position to clear the people from the west coast of Harris and by 1830 he had taken over Nisabost, Scarista and most of Seilebost and Borve. He had the remainder of these villages by the end of the 1830's. Perhaps the best comment on the man and his activities comes from Alexander Carmichael, the Gaelic scholar and folklore collector. In 1865 he visited the Island of Taransay and saw the inroads of the sea into a graveyard there. He made a note about it in his diary — "The tide being as ruthless as Stewart who had Losgaintir and who ploughed the cladh (graveyard) the people had at Seilebost, the oldest in Harris, till skulls and thigh bones etc. were rolling about on the surface of the ground like stones in a stony field, the ground being literally covered with them. These Stewarts were the greatest curse that ever came to Harris".

had excited a man like MacLeod to depart from the numerous promises of friendship and protection which he had offered. Stewart, a wretch in whom my uncle had uniformly confided, and who had till now manifested symptoms of regard and attachment, I well knew had been the principal cause of this, I had become obnoxious to him, because being a man of mean part & conscious of his ignorance he looked with jealousy and apprehension upon every person whom he suspected of knowing more than himself; and it had been whispered that I was to get the offices of Surgeon and Factor to the country. Besides I had treated him with the disrespect which I conceived his meanness merited. He had brothers too to assist - and was anxious to extend his possessions, and North Town was the finest farm in the country. The promises of the Laird were all that we had to depend upon. Those which he had made to my uncle were dissipated as I have said, and no hope longer remained with him. But I had taken care, during my late visits, to converse with the laird on the subject: and fortunately I had extorted promises from him of a binding nature, and which could not but be still fresh to his mind, of course the plea of remoteness was not to be sustained: and I would not be put off. I do not remember the words which I used, for in truth I was burning with indignation, but I repeated his promises and refuted every argument - Stewart said little; but I showed him I was not ignorant of his duplicity, by bringing forward one instance of it. Macleod had not the courage to deny his promises - Stewart though a great lump of a fellow, and a great blusterer among his vassals, is a coward - and so was completely silenced - and his patron was reduced to the necessity of concealing his agitation by having a prodigious dose of snuff - for he had not the courage to call me a liar, and without that his honour was likely to suffer. So they deemed it prudent to make it up with the party present, and after some preliminary concerns had been adjusted, gave a year of this farm, with the promise of a lease at the end of that time, if my uncle's affairs stood in good order. The rent £170. The person to whom the place had been promised for a year was Mr MacNiel of Kyles, for his sister Euphemia my Father's widow (not MacGillivray's mother). Mr MacLeod observed that he could put him off by refusing to recollect any promises made to him! Stewart hated the McNiels, and the giving them the farm was in all probability a stratagem for getting it ultimately into his own hands. However the MacNiels had used every effort to get my uncle put out. The first and most masterly stratagem was to demand immediate payment of a debt amounting to nearly £400, which had been allowed to lie dormant for several years.

Among others Mr Macleod mentioned that they had informed him my uncle was much in debt otherwise, that in particular he was due £40 to a merchant in Uist, and that either he and, or both of us had reported through the country that Mr Macleod was to be security for him in the case of the guardianship of his nephew, Donald. On coming out I contrived to get the MacNiels together. So we went to the public house, and represented the cruelty of urging payment at such a season, and the suspicious aspect which it wore and so on for the space of an hour. At parting we also got ourselves cleared of the imputation mentioned above - and the story of the debt was denied! My uncle and I dined in Donald MacDonald's. I ran to Mr Macleod's to inform him that we had cleared ourselves. He spoke as little as possible, and turned away without bidding goodbye - & so did I. He has been obliged to adhere to his promises in this case, though much against his will - and this is the cause of his displeasure. But I have happily gained a most important end, and strictly adhere to truth. So let his friendship go to the devil. I am mighty glad on't. After drinking some with Donald Macdonald we set off about eight o'clock - at Donald Ross's by the way we also took a tasting - and got home after ten.

Today I went to Borve, carrying some books for Mr Bethune and some verses for Miss Grant. I was very much pressed to stay all night - but managed to get off - and arrived at home about four o'clock.

Sunday, 12th April

The weather is improving yet we have nothing in flower but the Coltsfoot and the Daisy is in bud. Yesterday I went to Scarista with Mrs McG. I drank tea in the Ground-offices and saw Mr Macleod of Marig with James on their way to Rodill. He returned in the evening when I examined the Coltsfoot.

Monday.

Yesterday the weather was fine. We went to Scarista to hear Mr Macleod preach. His text was Matthew VI, 24. Through the whole discourse he had flat allusions to his own misfortunes in being deprived of Marig, and to the injustice of Macleod and his factor. He is but a lame preacher. The Bethunes were there, Miss Grant was confined with a headache - a great pity, thought I. Nothing of great importance occurred farther. In the dusk I walked to Lag-rainich and again to South town. Today the wind blew strongly first from the south and afterwards from the South west.

After breakfast I went over to the sand with the intention of going to Luskentir about my uncle's concerns. Mr MacLeod had agreed to give the farm only if Mr Stewart should find sufficient security for the payment of the rent in the stock upon it. We were anxious to know when Stewart intended to inspect it; and to find this out I was to go to Luskentir. Near Scarista I fell in with MacLeod & a gentleman unknown to me. He informed me that after our leaving Rodill, Roderick McNiel of Kyles had sent him a petition in which it was stated that his sister would be ruined if the farm was given to my uncle, observing that he could not comprehend how she should be ruined by the want of a thing which she never possessed. However a meeting between both parties had been appointed to take place at Rodill on Saturday first when it should be determined who was to have the farm. I make no comment on this. But it may be seen with what caution and security one should transact business with an unprincipled man. On the way home I shot a plover. Today I saw the Daisy in flower. The Wheatear is common. Last night I got a rotten specimen of a Fulmar which the shepherd had found at Moll-na-h'Ui, a fortnight ago. It resembles a gull very much. The whole plumage is lead colour tinged with red. Tail feathers 14. Under surface much lighter than the upper. The feet like those of a gull - only that in place of the hind toe is a mere nail. The under tail coverts nearly as long as the feathers. It agrees with the description by Linnous. At Rodill I saw the head and legs of an Eagle. They were much smaller than those of mine. The legs and beak were of a most beautiful pale orange - I could not determine which species they belonged to.

Tuesday.

A fine day. Went to Mas-na-beinne. On my return shot two plovers in Moll. In the evening found the Common Scurvy-grass in flower upon the walls of the Chapel of South town, which I, in course examined. Last night I began my poem, and hammered out twenty two lines of it. This evening I added sixteen, and after supper nineteen. I feel uneasy for want of employment, and must think upon something tomorrow with which to occupy myself.

Wednesday.

Weather coldish. Rose at nine. Before dinner (5 o'clock) I had added fifty verses to my poem - and after that 3 - concluding the introductory soliloquy.

Thursday.

Saw in the morning a very white Snow-bunting near the cornyard. After breakfast my uncle set out for Uist. The weather was very fine. I shot a gull on the sand, and found the Lesser Celandine and Common Whitlow-grass, the former in Allt-an-Liuir, the other on Tastir. In the evening we got intimation that Mr Stewart intended to inspect the stock tomorrow at ten o'clock. Before supper Mrs MacG sang some of my favourite songs - The Exile of Erin, Highland Mary, The Wounded Hussar, These groves of sweet myrtles, For lack of Gold, My Nanny O & c. I read part of De Luc's Elementary Treatise on Geology. Though the season is far advanced, vegetation has made little progress. On the sandy plains about the farm points of grass appear thinly scattered. Where the soil is black still less is seen. No seed of any kind has been sown on the farm, and only a small quantity of potatoes in some parts of the country.

Monday, 27th April, 1818

I have again become lethargic - unpardonably so. Since last report I have been at Pabbay, and at Caolas Uist about my uncle's business. He had got a year of the farm, but has not yet settled with the McNiels, and keeps one in the country till this be over. On my voyages I saw the Gannet in abundance, particularly in Caolas Bhearnaraidh, and an auk unknown to me I take to be the Razorbill. The transactions of last week, though well worth noting, I must pass over in silence because I have neglected to keep a regular account of them. For some days past I have been daily falling off from my former improved state. The causes of this I need not now trace; but must endeavour to regain what I have lost. From reading with considerable attention De Luc's Treatise on Geology I find that I need not be under the apprehension of ever exhausting those parts of the study of Nature which best suit my peculiar constitution. New subjects, I am persuaded will daily present themselves for investigation. The observation of Geological indices will henceforth occupy much of my time. On my way to Aberdeen I might acquire considerable mineralogical knowledge, if I possessed the necessary books and instruments - but in the deficiency of these I may even do something I shall at least become acquainted with a few species. I have not yet seen an account of the Birds of Britain with which I am entirely pleased; and I have of late been thinking upon the subject. Perhaps it might not be a mad scheme to attempt the Ornithology of Scotland. I certainly would not engage for more. But whether this alone would be acceptable I cannot yet determine. However I shall begin to note every particular regarding it, which I can observe, or collect from creditable authority. The time I occupy in this will not be misspent, even at the worst. For I will thus perhaps acquire habits of attention, observation, and activity. I shall probably spend a good deal of time in going through Skye - and I promise myself much pleasure from my wanderings there. I intend also to visit Ross, Sutherland, Caithness and Cromarty shires. But until my Uncle's affairs be reduced to order I cannot determine the plan which I am to follow. In the meantime let me begin my operations by a little drilling preparative to my entrance upon these designs. As I find that extreme cleanliness is conducive to bodily health and consequently to mental energy, I shall take care that it be attended to. This in particular for a beginning - for there are so many things to be noticed that I need not at present muster them in the form of a plan of conduct, but when I have begun they will present themselves in order, such is the fickleness of my mind, that my whole life, hitherto has been nothing else than a confused mass of error and repentance, amendment and relapse. But a period has at length arrived when I must lay aside much of my folly and act the part of a man. I am truly ashamed of myself, not to say anything worse - and if I do not amend now and that considerably I may fairly give up all efforts and just allow myself to be blown about by every circumstance that may occur.

Wednesday, 29th April, 1818
This was a day appointed by Roderick MacNiel of Kyles for a meeting between them and us, but no notice was sent, probably owing to the badness of the weather. For two or three days we have had southerly winds - previous to this, since the 6th the wind has been easterly, some days ago I saw a pair of Redwings near Drimafuind one of which I shot. From this it would seem likely that the species breeds here. I saw one about a week ago at South town. Today I saw two specimens of a sea bird very common here at certain seasons of the year and called Siolld. They were plucked however, so that I could not determine the species with accuracy. The genus is Mergus, and the species probably the Goosander. On Saturday I went with Rory Bethune to fish upon Loch Languad. I killed only one & he two. On Eilean-na-Caillich I saw a species of Willow in flower. I pocketed some sand of pure white quartz which I found on the shores of this lake. I have engaged Roderick to preserve a nest with

eggs of each species common in the country. They may be sent to Aberdeen by Stornoway.

Thursday - Chapel of South Town - Bencapval-

As I am about to undertake another journey or rather to begin the completion of my last I shall note some particulars regarding my present condition and thus close my Journal for the present. Tomorrow being the first day of summer, may very properly be made the first of a new account, and of a new mode of arranging matters, more especially as a reform is loudly called for.

In regard to the objects which I had in view on this trip, I may say that with the single exception of not having found specimens of the Itch insect, I have attained them in a greater or less degree. I have enjoyed for six months past an almost uninterrupted course of good health, more especially for the last three months, during which I have not even experienced a headache of half an hour's duration. Hence I infer that my constitution is mending. Perhaps with due care I may yet attain such firmness of frame as I might reasonably have expected, had not my own folly and a few adverse circumstances frustrated the intention of Nature. However, I am at present strongly fortified against the assault of every vitiating circumstance, and am there in as far as regards corporeal constitution well fitted for any exertion requisite in the study of nature. I find that a great deal of exercise is necessary for keeping me in health; and as I could not relinquish scientific pursuits I must endeavour to find some employment with which a high degree of mental gains an equal share of corporeal exertion. This among other reasons inclines me to follow the study of nature.

Since my arrival here I have made but few acquirements from want of books. The new studies in which I have engaged are mineralogy and Geology. With the morbidly irritable frame of body which I before possessed, I have perhaps lost a good deal of my mental sensibility. Of this however I am not certain, if an increasing tranquillity be a symptom of decreasing sensibility my apprehension would appear to be just. But this I am inclined to think may be attributed to other causes, such as good health, more rational ideas of things, and the heart easing effects of friendship.

My acquirements may be numerated in few words, of most of the physical sciences, I have got a smattering. In Geology I have made considerable progress, particularly in Ornithology. I have just begun the study of mineralogy. But Botany with which I began the study of Nature, and which I have cultivated for two years has been peculiarly captivating. Yet though I may be well acquainted with the principles and terms of the art I have not examined above 500 species.

On the fine arts, I may say I have bestowed considerable attention. Poetry is my favourite, and I am told that my performance is not quite despicable, and that I ought to pursue the study with unremitting attention. I am at times inclined to think so, but at others the fear of never attaining any considerable degree of merit in this department prevents me from occupying much of my time with it. For painting I have a natural genius, and in as far as I have tried this art I have succeeded well. Flower drawing however is the only branch of it in which I have made considerable progress. As to Music: I can just read an air with difficulty, with the Violin and German Flute, of its theory I know little or nothing.

Physiognomy as nearly related to Natural History has engaged my attention. Indeed I have been as much enamoured of it as of Botany. But my progress in the study of this art has been slow and interrupted, and after all I cannot say that I possess much more knowledge of it than a common person of tolerable education and some observation who has taken no pains to cultivate it as a science.

These are the departments of Science to which I am most inclined by nature - consequently those in which I ought to excel. There are many others which I have tried - some indeed in which I have made considerable progress.

In the study of Languages I have not done much. Besides having considerable knowledge of my vernacular tongue with its dialects, I have acquired the Gaelic, and studied the Latin, I also learned the rudimental part of the Greek and French languages: but have so much neglected both as today scarcely to know the letters of the former, and the derivation of a few words of the language mentioned from it; and of the latter I can just understand about two thirds of a passage on any ordinary subject. In Elocution I am told I have made great proficiency.

Of Medicine, including Anatomy, Physiology, Medicine proper, Surgery and Pharmacy, I know a little - and just a little - Chemistry as applicable to medicine engaged my attention. I have heard lectures on it, and studied it with some attention.

The other sciences of which I have just a smattering and nothing more are Mathematics, Philosophy natural and moral, and Agriculture. Of Civil History I know very little.

Thus I cannot boast of having acquired a thorough knowledge of any one science.

Yet I must confess I am in a fair way - and if I can but acquire habits of industry and assiduity, may before the end of four or five years be eminent in something. I have certainly laid a good foundation - and the knowledge which I possess of so many sciences, little as it is, will enable me with greater ease and certainty to excel in any one of them, or in any other.

Note on the colour plates.
MacGillivray's second son, Paul Howard MacGillivray, went to Australia after his father's death, and became a successful surgeon in Melbourne. He took with him his father's paintings and probably his journals. Paul returned the paintings to the Natural History Museum in London in 1892, where they remain to this day. There are 213 watercolours of birds, mammals, and fishes, 122 of them of birds. Although they were painted in the 1830s, a decade or more after this journal was written, a small number have been reproduced here as an example of MacGillivray's artistic talent. The pictures selected are all of species that he would have seen on Harris.

Lesser Black-backed Gull

Blackbird

Short-eared Owl

Oystercatcher

Kestrel

Common Tern

Common Sandpiper

The landscape view is from the shoulder of Chaipaval above the old farmhouse of North Town, looking across Bun an Ois and Northton sands to Scarista and the hills of North Harris.

Postscript

When MacGillivray left Northton to return to Aberdeen he intended to walk through Skye, Ross-shire, Sutherland and Caithness, to see parts of the country he hadn't visited. There is no evidence to show whether or not he made the journey. After his death in 1852, many of MacGillivray's papers, his journals, and his paintings, were taken to Australia by his second son, Paul Howard MacGillivray, who became a well-known surgeon in Melbourne. He sent his father's paintings back to the Natural History Museum in London, where they are to this day, but there are none of MacGillivray's journals or papers in any Australian library or museum. There was a major library fire in Sydney in the 1890s and it seems probable that his journals, which would have covered his walk through the Highlands after leaving Northton, were destroyed there. There is not a great deal of information to show what MacGillivray did in the ten years after his stay in Northton. In 1819 he was teaching a botany class in Aberdeen and in the autumn of that year he made a remarkable journey to London. The best collection of birds in Britain was in the British Museum and MacGillivray decided that he should see it; he walked from Aberdeen to London so that he could see the countryside along the way. The direct route from Aberdeen to London is a little over 500 miles but MacGillivray walked 801 miles in just over eight weeks. He walked 500 miles through Scotland before he crossed the border into England at Carlisle, 500 miles in which he visited parts of Scotland that he hadn't seen before. Fortunately the journal he kept along the way has survived, and as with his Northton journal, in it there are long lists of the plants and birds that he saw along the way.

His experience at the British Museum made him determined to become an ornithologist and publish an account of the birds of Scotland. On the 29th September 1820 he returned to Northton to marry Marion MacAskill, he was 24, she was 17. There is no information covering the next year or two, on where he and Marion lived, or how he made money, but in 1823 MacGillivray was appointed as an assistant and secretary to Professor Robert Jameson, the Regius Professor of Natural History in Edinburgh. Jameson had one of the biggest collections of natural history specimens in the country and part of MacGillivray's job was to help curate it. Jameson was a difficult man to work with and it seems likely that he and MacGillivray parted company after a few years, and MacGillivray was left to support himself by writing articles and by translating French and German texts. In 1831 he was appointed as Conservator of the Museum of the Royal College of Surgeons in Edinburgh, a post he held very successfully for ten years. The 1830s were an important decade for MacGillivray. He published his first book, a botanical text, in 1830 and this was followed by many others, on geology, on ornithology, on scientific biography, but most importantly by the first three volumes of his monumental *History of British Birds*. However the most significant event was in 1830 when MacGillivray was introduced to John James Audubon, the famous American bird artist. The two men became life-long friends, a friendship that laid the foundations of ornithology in Britain and the United States. Audubon had already embarked on his remarkable paintings *The Birds of America*, and MacGillivray was a considerable help to him in producing the text to accompany the paintings, the *Ornithological Biographies*. There is no doubt that Audubon was a considerable influence on MacGillivray's paintings. They are very similar in style to Audubon's and Audubon himself regarded them very highly. They were meant to accompany the *History of British Birds* but sadly MacGillivray could never afford to have his paintings engraved and published.

In 1841 MacGillivray went back to Aberdeen, his native city, as the Regius Professor of Natural History at Marischal College, a remarkable achievement considering the humble circumstances of his birth. He was a popular enthusiastic teacher, well loved by his students, but he also carried on publishing, a book on molluscs and the last two volumes of the *History of British Birds*. His last years were not especially happy ones. There was always money to worry about and his health broke down in the autumn of 1850. Marion, his wife, died in February 1852, aged 47, and MacGillivray himself died in September of the same year, aged 56.

MacGillivray has never received the credit and acknowledgement that his efforts as a naturalist and an artist merit. There are probably several reasons for this. When he was a student in Edinburgh Charles Darwin met MacGillivray and wrote that he "treated me kindly but had not the manners of a gentleman". This did not seem to bother Darwin who made considerable use of MacGillivray's work when developing his own ideas, but MacGillivray's forthright opinions upset many of the gentleman-naturalists of the day. He also developed his own unorthodox scheme of bird classification, a scheme that received little support, and in fact was flawed, but perhaps the main reason for neglecting MacGillivray is that he worked in the years before Darwin published *On the Origin of Species* in 1859 and this has cast a great shadow over everyone who went before.

Above all else MacGillivray deserves to be remembered as Scotland's, perhaps Britain's, greatest field naturalist. Even today, someone interested in the behaviour or habits of a British bird could benefit by seeing what MacGillivray has to say about it. Darwin, when using one of MacGillivray's field observations, referred to him as "the accurate MacGillivray", an accuracy of recording and insistence on the truth, the early development of which runs through his Northton journal.

APPENDIX I

MacGillivray compiled several long lists of plants that he had recorded while walking from Aberdeen. It is a measure of MacGillivray's character and calibre as a field naturalist that he was able to walk more than 30 miles in a day and in the evening sit down and record, using their Latin names, all of the plants that he had seen. He was an accomplished botanist and in 1830 he published a revised version of Withering's *A Systematic Arrangement of British Plants*, a very successful book that ran to 13 editions over the next 30 years.

The English names that I have used for these plants are the names that MacGillivray would have used; I have taken them from an edition of his own botanical book. In most cases they are the same as today's familar names.

The plants seen between the Glens of Foudland and Fochabers, during a walk of 35 miles.

Veronica officinalis Common Speedwell
Anthyllis vulneraria Kidney Vetch
Lotus corniculatus Common Bird's-foot Trefoil
Prunella vulgaris Self-heal
Euphrasia officinalis Eye-bright
Cynosurus cristatus Crested Dog's-tail-grass
Trifolium repens White Trefoil
Erica cinerea Common Heath
Senecio aquaticus Marsh Ragwort
Bromus mollis Soft Broom-grass
Erica vulgaris Common Ling
Lychnis flos-cuculi Ragged Robin
Anthoxanthum odoratum Sweet-scented Spring-grass
Erica tetralix Cross-leaved Heath
Pedicularis palustris Marsh Lousewort
Tormentilla officinalis Common Tormentil Septfoil
Plantago lanceolata Ribwort Plaintain
Eriophorum angustifolia Common Cotton-grass
Carduus palustris Marsh Thistle

Bellis perennis Common Daisy

Alchemilla vulgaris Common Lady's Mantle

Plantago media Hoary Plantain

Galeopsis tetrahit Common Hemp-nettle

Galium erectum Upright Bedstraw

Veronica chamaedrys Germander Speedwell

Galeopsis versicolor Large-flowered Hemp-nettle

Trifolium pratense Common Purple Clover

Juncus squarrosus Moss Rush

Carduus lanceolatus Spear Thistle

Geranium molle Common Dove's-foot Crane's-bill

Nardus stricta Mat-grass

Juncus conglomeratus Common Rush

Hypericum pulchrum Small Upright St. John's-wort

Myosotis palustris Great Water Scorpion Grass

Juncus effusus Soft Rush

Viola tricolor Pansy Violet

Rhinanthus crista galli Yellow Rattle

Ranunculus repens Creeping Crowfoot

Cerastium viscosum Narrow-leaved Mouse-eared Chickweed

Spergula arvensis Corn Spurrey

Ranunculus acris Upright Meadow Crowfoot

Cerastium vulgatum Broad-leaved Chickweed

Achillea ptarmica Sneeze-wort

Senecio Jacobaea Common Ragwort

Rumex acetosa Common Sorrel

Cardamine pratensis Ladies' Smock

Achillea millefolium Common Yarrow

Holcus avenaceus Oat-like Soft-grass

Stellaria media Common Chickweed

Bunium flexuosum Earth-nut

Polygala vulgaris Common Milkwort

Raphanus raphanistrum Charlock

Vicia sepium Common Bush Vetch

Lapsana communis Common Nipple-wort

Matricaria chamomilla Common Wild Chamomile
Orobus tuberosus Heath Pea
Vicia cracca Tufted Vetch
Montia fontana Water Chickweed
Lathyrus pratensis Yellow Meadow Vetchling
Hieracium murorum Broad-leaved Wall Hawkweeed
Stellaria uliginosa Bog Stitchwort
Polygonum aviculare Common Knot-grass
Thymus serpyllum Wild Thyme
Gnaphalium dioicum Mountain Cudweed
Scleranthus annuus Annual Knawel
Ranunculus aquaticus Water Crowfoot
Rumex acetosella Sheep's Sorrel
Lycopodium clavatum Common Clubmoss
Rosa villosa Soft-leaved Round-fruited Rose
Orchis maculata Spotted Palmate Orchid
Campanula rotundifolia Round-leaved Bell-flower
Carduus arvensis Field Thistle
Rumex crispus Curley Dock
Centaurea cyanus Corn Blue-bottle
Spiraea ulmaria Meadow Sweet
Rosa spinosissima Burnet Rose
Comarum palustre Marsh Cinque-foil
Briza minor Little Quaking Grass
Linum catharticum Purging Flax
Sparganium ramosum Branched Bur-reed
Vicia sylvatica Wood Vetch
Centaurea nigra Black Knapweed
Plantago maritima Sea Plantain
Pteris aquilina Common Brake

The *Briza minor* (Little Quaking Grass) was found in great abundance on the side of a brae by the Old Huntly road about one mile and a quarter from Keith. The *Vicia sylvatica* (Wood Vetch) in a deep gullet between the second & third mile stones from Fochabers on the Keith road.

The plants seen between Fochabers and Forres.

Geranium robertianum Herb Robert

Centaurea Cyanus Corn Blue-bottle

Rumex crispus Curled Dock

Erysimum officinale Treacle Mustard

Centaurea nigra Black Knapweed

Achillea ptarmica Sneeze-wort

Sambucus nigra Common Elder

Campanula rotundifolia Round-leaved Bell Flower

Pteris aquilina Common Brake

Rubus fruticosus Common Bramble

Achillea millefolium Common Yarrow

Euphrasia officinalis Eyebright

Digitalis purpurea Foxglove

Veronica chamadrys Germander Speedwell

Ranunculus flamma Lesser Spearwort

Urtica dioica Great Nettle

Lycopsis arvensis Small Bugloss

Erica cinerea Common Heath

Urtica urens Small Nettle

Polygonum convolvulus Black Bindweed

Erica vulgaris Common Ling

Bellis perennis Common Daisy

Vicia sativa Common Vetch

Tormentilla officinalis Common Tormentil Septfoil

Carduus arvensis Field Thistle

Galeopsis versicolor Large-flowered Hemp-nettle

Lotus corniculatus Common Bird's-foot Trefoil

Viola tricolor Pansy Violet

Chrysanthemum segmentum Corn Marigold

Gnaphalium dioicum Mountain cud-weed

Vicia cracca Tufted Vetch

Prunella vulgaris Self-heal

Erica tetralix Cross-leaved Heath

Cerastium viscosum Narrow-leaved Mouse-eared Chickweed
Hypericum pulchrum Small Upright St. John's Wort
Senecio jacobaea Common Ragwort
Rananculus repens Creeping Crowfoot
Rumex acetosa Common Sorrel
Arctium lappa Burdock
Hieracium murorum Broad-leaved Wall Hawkweed
Trifolium repens White Trefoil
Polygonum aviculare Common Knot-grass
Veronica officinalis Common Speedwell
Trifolium pratense Common Purple Clover
Myosotis versicolor Yellow Scorpion Grass
Orchis maculata Spotted Palmate Orchid
Spergula arvensis Corn Spurrey
Agrostemma githago Corn Cockle
Polygala vulgaris Common Milkwort
Galium verum Common Yellow Bedstraw
Plantago media Hoary Plantain
Carduus nutans Musk Thistle
Plantago maritima Sea Plantain
Galium erectrum Upright Bedstraw
Matricaria chamoma Common Wild Chamomile
Plantago lanceolata Ribwort Plantain
Galium aparine Goose Grass
Lathyrus pratensis Yellow Meadow Vetchling
Spirea ulmaria Meadow Sweet
Thlaspi Bursa-pastoris Common Shepherd's Purse
Eriophorum angustifolia Common Cotton-grass
Juncus conglomeratus Common Rush
Valeriana officinalis Great Wild Valerian
Rhinanthus crista galli Yellow Rattle
Juncus effusus Soft Rush
Polygonum persicaria Spotted Persicaria
Senecio viscosus Stinking Groundsel
Juncus squarrosus Moss Rush

Orobus tuberosus Heath Pea

Senecio vulgaris Common Groundsel

Ervum hirsutum Hairy Tare

Rumex acetosella Sheep's Sorrel

Senecio aquaticus Marsh Ragwort

Erodium cicutarium Hemlock Stork's Bill

Malva sylvestris Common Mallow

Carduus lanceolatus Spear Thistle

Lapsana communis Common Nipple-wort

Anthyllis vulneraria Kidney-vetch

Papavar dubium Long Smooth-headed Poppy

Geranium molle Common Dove's-foot Crane's-bill

Ononis arvensis Rest-harrow

Genista anglica Needle Green-weed

Leontodon taraxacum Common Dandelion

Heracleum sphondylium Cow-parsnip

Linum catharticum Purging Flax

Asplenium ruta-muraria Wall-rue Spleenwort

Fumaria officinalis Common Fumitory

The plants seen between Forres and Inverness.

Malva sylvestris Comon Mallow

Erysimum officinale Treacle Mustard

Galium erectum Upright Bedstraw

Matricaria chamomilla Common Wild Chamomile

Trifolium repens White Trefoil

Lotus corniculatus Common Bird's-foot Trefoil

Bellis perennis Common Daisy

Sedum sexangulare Insipid Yellow Stonecrop

Galium verum Common Yellow Bedstraw

Rumex acetosa Common Sorrel

Rhinanthus Crista galli Yellow Rattle

Senecio jacobaea Common Ragwort

Stellaria media Common Chickweed

Erodium cicutarium Hemlock Stork's-bill

Urtica dioica Great Nettle

Anthyllis vulneria Kidney-vetch

Polygonum aviculare Common Knot-grass

Ranunculus repens Crawling Crow's-foot

Arctium lappa Burdock

Polygala vulgaris Common Milkwort

Achillaea millefolium Common Yarrow

Carduus palustris Marsh Thistle

Thlaspi Bursa-pastoris Common Shepherd's Purse

Carduus lanceolatus Spear Thistle

Scabiosa succisa Devil's-bit Scabious

Lamium purpureum Red Dead-nettle

Vicia cracca Tufted Vetch

Ervum hirsutum Hairy Tare

Sinapis arvensis Field Mustard

Geranium molle Common Dove's-foot Crane's-bill

Senecio aquaticus Marsh Ragwort

Senecio vulgaris Common Groundsel

Centaurea Cyanus Corn Blue-bottle

Euphrasia officinalis Eyebright

Sonchus arvensis Corn Sow-thistle

Juncus effusus Soft Rush

Agrostemma Githdgo Corn Cockle

Campanula rotundifolia Round-leaved Bell Flower

Juncus conglomeratus Common Rush

Papaver dubium Long Smooth-headed Poppy

Juncus squarrosus Moss Rush

Achillea Millefolium Common Yarrow

Centaurea nigra Black Knapweed

Tormentilla officinalis Common Tormentil Septfoil

Cerastium vulgatum Broad-leaved Mouse-eared Chickweed

Lycopsis arvensis Small Bugloss

Spergula arvensis Corn Spurrey

Galium Aparine Goose Grass

Fumaria claviculata Fumitory

Galeopsis versicolor Large Flowered Hemp-nettle

Rumex acetosella Sheep's Sorrel

Lithospermum arvense Corn Gromwell

Lamium amplexicaule Hen-bit Dead-nettle

Cerastium viscosum Narrow-leaved Mouse-eared Chickweed

Raphanus Raphanistranum Field Radish

Trifolium filiforme Slender Yellow Trefoil

Myosotis versicolor Yellow Scorpion-grass

Gnaphalium dioicum Mountain Cud-weed

Plantago maritima Sea Plantain

Rumex crispus Curled Dock

Ononis arvensis Rest-harrow

Polygonum Convolvulus Black Bindweed

Hieracium murorum Broad-leaved Wall Hawk-weed

Rosa spinosissima Burnet Rose

Plantago media Hoary Plantain

Prunella vulgaris Self-heal

Rosa canina Dog Rose

Genista anglica Needle Green-weed

Achillea ptarmica Sneeze-wort

Rubus fruticosus Common Bramble

Gentiana campestris Field Gentian

Trifolium pratense Common Purple Clover

Hypericum pulchrum Small Upright St. John's Wort

Potentilla anserina Silver-weed

Myosotis palustris Great water Scorpion-grass

Cardamine pratensis Ladies' Smock

Potentilla anserina Silver-weed

Polygonum persicaria Spotted Persicaria

Euphorbia helioscopia Sun Spurge

Epilobium palustre Round-stalked Marsh Willow-herb

Scleranthus annuus Annual Knawel

Lapsana communis Common Nipple-wort

Vicia sativa Common Vetch

Ranunculus flamma Lesser Spear-wort
Sedum acre Biting Stonecrop
Linum catharticum Purging Flax
Erica vulgaris Common Ling
Thymus serpyllum Wild Thyme
Pteris aquilina Common Brake
Erica tetralix Cross-leaved Heath
Senecio viscosus Stinking Groundsel
Hieracium pilosella Mouse-ear Hawkweed
Erica cinerea Common Heath
Bartsia odontites Red Bartsia
Pedicularis sylvatica Common Lousewort
Veronica beccabunga Short-leaved Water Speedwell
Orchis maculata Spotted Palmate Orchid
Alchemilla arvensis Parsley Piert
Plantago Major Greater Plantain
Statice Armeria Common Thrift
Heracleum Sphondylium Cow-parsnip
Spirea Ulmaria Meadow Sweet
Silene maritima Sea Campion
Viola tricolor Pansy Violet
Cochlearia officinalis Common Scurvy-grass
Chrysanthemum segetum Corn Marigold

The plants found on the south side of Loch Ness.

Rubus corylifolius Hazle-leaved Bramble
Ranunculus repens Creeping Crowfoot
Ranunculus hederaceus Ivy-leaved Crowfoot
Galium verum Common Yellow Bedstraw
Gentiana campestris Field Gentian
Rosa canina Common Dog Rose
Euphrasia officinalis Eyebright
Bellis perennis Common Daisy
Urtica dioica Great Nettle

Rosa tomentosa Downy-leaved Dog Rose

Geranium Robertum Herb Robert

Prunella vulgaris Self Heal

Myosotis versicolor Yellow Scorpion-grass

Campanula rotundifolia Round-leaved Bell Flower

Spirea ulmaria Meadow Sweet

Centaurea nigra Black Knapweed

Plantago lanceolata Ribwort Plantain

Plantago maritima Sea Plantain

Senecio Jacobea Common Ragwort

Juncus conglomeratus Common Rush

Carduus palustris Marsh Thistle

Veronica Beccabunga Short-leaved Water Speedwell

Ranunculus Flammula Lesser Spearwort

Trifolium repens White Trefoil

Stachys sylvatica Hedge Woundwort

Of these the Mountain Globe-flower, Wood Vetch and Saw-wort cannot be properly said to grow on the banks. The first having been found in the romantic valley of Alt mor, the others at the Fall of Foyers.

The plants out of flower which I observed were the;

Juniperus communis Common Juniper

Fragaria vesca Wood Strawberry

Betula alba White Birch

Rubus idaeus Raspberry Bush

Geum rivale Water Avens

Tussilago Farfara Colt's-foot

Primula vulgaris Common Primrose

Quercus Robur Common Oak

Ulex europaeus Common Gorse

Oxalis acetosella Common Wood-sorrel

Fraxinus excelsior Common Ash

Mercurialis perennis Perennial Mercury

Pinus sylvestris Scotch Fir
Orchis maculata Spotted Palmate Orchid
Asperula odorata Sweet Woodruff
Corylus Avellana Common Hazel
Pinguicula vulgaris Common Butterwort
Bunium flexuosum Earth-nut
Prunus spinosa Sloe-tree
Stellaria holostea Greater Stitchwort

The Scotch Fir we only saw on the rocks at the Fall, and even there, were but three or four specimens. It has a peculiarly fine effect in highland scenery, but loses it entirely when cultivated, or disposed in such woods as we find in the Lowlands.

The plants seen from Muir of Ord to Scatwell on the river Conan, about 8 miles.

Silene maritima Sea Campion
Anthyllis vulneraria Kidney-vetch
Scabiosa succisa Devil's-bit Scabious
Alchemilla alpina Alpine Lady's Mantle
Narthecium ossifragum Bog Asphodel
Ranunculus Flamma Lesser Spear-wort
Gentiana campestris Field Gentian
Achillaea Millefolium Common Yarrow
Trifolium repens White Trefoil
Achillaea ptarmica Sneeze-wort
Tormentilla officinalis Common Tormentil Septfoil
Solidago Virgaurea Common Golden Rod
Carduus lanceolatus Spear Thistle
Rosa canina Common Dog Rose
Galium verum Common Yellow Bedstraw
Prunella vulgaris Self-heal
Spiraea Ulmaria Meadow-sweet
Lotus corniculatus Common Bird's-foot Trefoil
Ranunculus repens Creeping Crowfoot

Valeriana officinalis Great Wild Valerian

Erica vulgaris Common Ling

Plantago lanceolata Ribwort Plantain

Erica tetralix Cross-leaved Heath

Chrysanthemum segmentum Corn Marigold

Teucrium scorodonia Wood Sage

Erica cinerea Common Heath

Spergula arvensis Corn Spurrey

Pteris aquilina Common Brake

Trifolium pratense Common Purple Clover

Galeopsis versicolor Large-flowered Hemp-nettle

Plantago maritima Sea Plantain

Rhinanthus crista-galli Yellow Rattle

Cerastium viscosum Narrow-leaved Mouse-eared Chickweed

Campanula rotundifolia Round-leaved Bell Flower

Euphrasia officinalis Eyebright

Rumex Acetosa Common Sorrel

APPENDIX II

Harris

At the period of MacGillivray's Journal, the Isle of Harris was entering a period of change which was to end in the destruction of almost all of its original communities.

In 1778 Harris had been sold by MacLeod of Harris to his cousin Captain Alexander MacLeod of Berneray, who invested great sums of money in setting up a new fishing industry, centred around his new piers and harbour at Rodel. Fishermen were brought in from all over the Western Isles, and even from the Scottish mainland, to settle in the new fishing villages along the east coast of the Island. Between this commercial fishing, and the kelp industry, providing scarce chemicals from seaweed at the time of the French Wars, the economy of Harris entered a period of boom. Even if rents had been inflated in line with the kelp boom, there was still plenty of employment to provide wages with which to pay them.

Many of the villages of the machairs of West Harris had been held as joint-tenancies by groups of local people, but as the kelp trade failed after the end of the French Wars, it became more difficult to pay the higher rents, and they fell into arrears. By the time of the Journal, the townships of Horgabost and Nisabost had been cleared to make a farm, and the townships of South Town, Uidh and Druim a' Phuinnd had been cleared and added to North Town. In North Harris, all the villages west of Ardhasaig had been cleared, and their land leased as sheep-farms. Within twenty years of the Journal, Scarista, the Borves, Seilebost - every village in West Harris - would be cleared, and added to the farms of MacRa and Stewart.

Now it was the turn of the farms - these had for generations been let to cadet families of the MacLeods, but the landlords had ceased to look on their tacksmen - tenants under long lease - as part of a family group, but had come to look more to the commercial value of their lands. By the time of the Journal, North Town had been let to the MacGillivrays, who are said to have come from the boundaries of Inverness and Aberdeen counties, while Husinish and much of North Harris had passed as a sheep farm to Alexander MacRa from Kintail. Luskentyre had been let to Donald Stewart, and he was looking to extend his farms to include the rest of West Harris.

By the end of the Journal, Stewart and young MacLeod, the grandson of Captain Alexander, are scheming to remove the MacGillivrays from Northton in favour of the MacNeils of Kyles, but, as young William realises, the plan is in the long term to give it to Stewart or MacRa. Although William manages to ward off the change for a year, the farm will eventually pass to MacRa, and he and Stewart will between them have every worthwhile piece of land on Harris.

Glossary of Places and Persons

General Note
MacGillivray's Gaelic spelling was idiosyncratic and frequently inconsistent, so his versions of names throughout the Journal may not always be exactly the same as those in the Glossary.

Part 1 Places

Allt an Liuir   A little stream on Chaipaval, running north from above the Liuri.
Amhin Shorsaidh   River Housay on OS maps - one of the rivers running into the head of Loch Resort.
Ard Ghreotinis   Ard Groadnish - a headland behind Luskentyre Farm and site of another Dun or Iron Age watch tower.
Ardhasig   Ardhasaig - a village on a headland in West Loch Tarbert, below the Clisham.
Avin Laidhnis   Abhainn Laidhnis - a stream on the north-east corner of Chaipaval.
Baile Nicoll   A former township in Uig, now part of Ardroil.
Balla mhic ic Ioin bhan   In the context, this name may be fictitious, but it might be a detail of the scenery around Luachair whose name has been forgotten or changed. "Balla" may stand for Baile, a town, but it could also mean a ledge on a cliff, in which case the meaning would be the ledge of the grandson of Fair John.
Balnakill   The site of the Church and Manse of Uig, near Timsgarry.
Bealach an Sgail   The pass leading north from Bunabhainneadarra, between the Clisham and Uisgnaval, into Glen Langadal.
Ben Capval   Now more commonly Chaipaval, the hill on the peninsula of Toe Head. Said to be from the Norse, signifying bow-shaped hill, which is certainly its appearance from Scarista.
Ben Luskentir   A massif of hill stretching almost across the width of Harris, which has to be either ascended or circumvented on the way north toTarbert. The old route led from Luskentyre along Glen Laxdale to Geirisdale, then climbed across the shoulder of Ben Luskentyre between Beinn nan Leac and Uaval Mor, through the pass of Beul na Bearnadh, then dropping down by Cadha nan Each (the pass of the horses) behind Ceanndibig, and proceeding either to Tarbert, or to the old village of Stioclett, thence by boat to North Harris.

Bernera   Great Bernera, an island in Loch Roag, Lewis, as distinct from Berneray in the Sound of Harris.

Berneray   A populous island in the Sound of Harris, and the only one still inhabited. The home of the MacLeods of Berneray, who included Sir Norman, knighted at the Battle of Worcester, Donald who took an honourable part in the '45 rebellion, and Captain Alexander who became the proprietor of Harris.

Blue Cave on Ui   A cave on the west side of the Uidh at Northton.

Borve   A group of three villages - Big, Middle and Little Borve - on the west coast of Harris, cleared for sheep in 1838. The name derives from the Norse Borg, and refers to the iron age fort, or Dun, on a rock outcrop behind the village.

Boter   Not identified, but the context would suggest the shieling village of Bolabrat, in a valley on the shoulder of Chaipaval behind the farmhouse of North Town.

Brew House   Pabbay was famous for the production of illicit whisky. This was used as the excuse for the clearance of the island in 1842.

Builibhal   The hill behind Borve in West Harris.

Bun-abhainn-edir   Bunabhainneadarra - literally "the mouth of the river in between" - a village on West Loch Tarbert opposite Ardhasaig. Later the site of a whaling station.

Bun an Ois   The mouth of the stream which flows from the head of Northton Bay (Traigh an Taoibh Tuath) across the sands. Care has to to be taken crossing here at flood-tide, because of quicksands.

Caolas Bhearnaraidh   The Sound of Berneray, between Berneray and North Uist.

Caolas Stocnis   A township on the east coast of Harris; one of many set up by Captain Alexander MacLeod of Berneray in the days of the fishing stations in the 1780s. Stockinish Island has a large natural sea-pond, which was at one time used as a lobster-pond. It is now a major harbour for fish farming etc.

Capdal   A former village in Uig, also now part of Ardroil.

Carnach Bhan   Presumably the same as the present Bealach Ban, the gully leading from the top of Chaipaval to the site of the farmhouse.

Carnan mhic Thasgill   The steep slope leading from the present Northton towards Obbe. The identity of the MacAskill after whom it was named is not known.

Carnis   Carnish - a township in Uig west of Ardroil.

Carn Uilliam   Not used today, but from the context a cairn built on the top of Chaipaval, and named after some William - possibly even MacGillivray himself.

Cave (p51)   Uamh Ulladail - the cave of Ulladale - in which Donald MacLeod of Berneray hid for a time after the Battle of Culloden.

Ceann Dibig   A village a few miles south of Tarbert on the east coast. At the time of the Journal it was a boundary shepherds' village, but it was later crofted.

Ceann na Sgeiradh   A headland at the east end of the Scarista Beach; also called Sgeir Liath - the grey rock.

Clisham   The highest mountain in Harris. Most Harris hills have Norse names ending in -val, but the name Clisham may predate even the Norse period. Its meaning, and even its language, are still the subject of controversy.

Copay   Coppay - an island at the entrance to the Sound of Harris, on the west side of Chaipaval.

Coran   In this case probably Corran Sheileboist, the spit of sand running towards Luskentyre from Seilebost, but Corran Raa on Taransay is also a possibility.

Cosladir   Cosletter, the glen leading from Northton to Obbe.

Craco   Crago, the eastern part of the township of Seilebost.

Crallasta   Crowlista - a township in Uig near Timsgarry.

Creag Bheist   This name is not clear in the Journal, but presumably a rock outcrop, and probably near the head of Gleann Rodil.

Creag Camna   The western corner of the Maodal, recently used as a road metal quarry.

Dire Mor etc (p97)   A grouping of names in the North Harris Hills, of varying importance, included mainly for the sound of their names in Gaelic.

Dò   For Tobha, or Toe Head. Tobha means a prominent hill sticking out into the sea so Toe Head is a duplication of the name.

Drimafuinnd   Druim a' Phuinnd. The ridge of the pound, the site of the pens where stock straying on to the farm of North Town were impounded.

Druim nan Caorach   The hill-slope above the north west shore of Loch Langavat in Harris.

Drumisgarry   An odd version of Timsgarry.

Eilean na Caillich   An island at the west end of Loch Langavat, said to be the burial place of a nun, but cailleach can also mean a witch, or just any old woman!

Ensay   A very fertile island in the Sound of Harris, later occupied by the Stewarts of Luskentyre as a farm.

Erista   A former township in Uig, near Timsgarry.

Feadan Bhalaidh   Not a name in use today, but the context makes it clear that it is in the region of Brethasker, the low broken shore ground below the western slopes of Chaipaval.

Gasker   An island to the west of Taransay.

Geoth an Do   Geodha an Tobha - the gully on the point of Toe Head.

Gleann a' Chlair   The glen running southeast from the head of Loch Resort.

Gleann Bheagadil   Vigadale - a glen running east from above the head of Loch Langavat into Loch Seaforth.

Glen Langadal   A deep glen leading from below the Clisham to Loch Langavat on the Lewis border.

Glen Staoladil   Stuladal, a side glen on the path between Bealach a' Sgail and Luachair, above Loch Voshimid.

Haskir   An island to the west of Ru Griminish in North Uist.

Hirta   St Kilda, a group of islands lying in the Atlantic some fifty miles west of South Town.

Inis-shi   Nisishee - a cottar village on the boundary between Scarista and Northton.

Killigray   An island in the Sound of Harris, held by the Campbells as a farm along with the shorelands of Strond.

Kinrezort   The house on the Lewis side of the head of Loch Resort, usually occupied by a gamekeeper.

Kiose   Keose, in the Parish of Lochs. At the time of the Journal, the site of the Manse of Lochs.

Kirktown   Pabbay island at one time comprised four townships - Baile mu Thuath or North Town, Baile Meadhanach or Mid Town, Baile Lingay and Baile na Cille or Kirk Town. By the time of the Journal Baile mu Thuath, Baile Meadhanach and Lingay were all part of the farm of William MacNeil, while most of the Baile na Cille was in crofts.

Kyles (p53)   In this context Kyles Stiadar, the old ferry port on the coast between Northton and Obbe.

Kyles (p39)   In this context Kyles Berneray, a tack on the north shore of North Uist.

Lag Rainich   This would mean the valley of bracken, and could apply to one of the steep gullies on the west face of Chaipaval, above the Teampull.

Learadh Cove   Not identified.

Linach   Not a name in use now, but seems to apply to the flooded area at the mouth of the Lingay stream.

Liuir   Liuri - a dangerous concave cliff on the west side of Chaipaval, full of nesting sea-birds in the spring and summer.

Loch an Fheoir   In this context, one of the little lochs behind Loch Steisevat at Obbe.

Loch Languad (p31)   Langavat, a loch to the north of Roneval - from the Norse lang vatn - Long Loch.

Loch Languad (p50)   Another Loch Langavat, this time on the Lewis boundary.

Loch Leosabhidh   The sheltered sea loch at Abhainnsuidhe.

Loch na Cartach   A loch in the moor between Borve and Loch Langavat in Harris.

Loch na Morchadh   A loch behind Obbe, on the road to Loch Langavat.

Loch Rezort   Loch Resort, the western boundary between Harris and Lewis.

Loch Rog   Properly the whole sea-loch surrounding the island of Bernera, Lewis, but in this context Little Loch Roag, a narrow inlet from the main loch, which runs inland towards the lodge at Morsgail.

Loch Seaforth   A major sea-loch running north from East Loch Tarbert. The boundary between Lewis and Harris at this point. Its name probably derives from Sja Fjord - the pent-up fiord, as the upper part of the loch is dammed at lower tides by a rock barrier, near Airidhbhruaich.

Loch Suainnebhal   Suainavat - a large loch in Uig, running inland from behind Ardroil.

Lon of Moll   Lon is a marsh, so presumably the marshy land behind the Mol on the east side of Chaipaval.

Luachar   A village in Harris near the head of Loch Resort, the boundary between Lewis and Harris on the west side.

Luskentir   Luskentyre, a farm on the west side of Harris, but at this time including the whole of Ben Luskentyre, over to the Minch coast at Ceanndibig.

MacLellan's Park   The farm of Ensay, tenanted by Duncan MacLellan, included this land on the Uidh, probably a remnant of the days when the Teampull was the Parish Church of Harris, and the Minister lived on Ensay.

Maodal   A hill above the north-east corner of Northton Sands. An excellent viewpoint, and the site, a few years ago, of a fatal plane crash.

Marig   Now Maraig. Then a farm near the boundary of Lewis and Harris, but now a crofting township.

Mas na Beinnadh   Mas na Beinne - the foot of the hill. Usually referring to the lower ground on the furthest north point of Toe Head.

Miavag   Miabhag nam Beann in North Harris, as opposed to Miabhag nam Bagh, on the east coast.

Mill (p33)   The old mill of South Harris was situated at Obbe, near the present An Clachan, and the mill pond is still a popular spot for salmon fishing.

Moll   The stony beach on the east shore of Chaipaval, sometimes called Mol Leomadal to distinguish it from Mol na h-Uidhe.

Mol na h-Uidhe   The stony beach at Traigh na h-Uidhe, which is exposed after some heavy tides.

Nisbost   Nisabost, part of the present village of Horgabost.

North Town   The original farm of North Town, as distinguished from the South Town, was on the east facing side of Chaipaval, and had been a farm for many generations. By the time of the Journal, it had been amalgamated with the cleared villages of Southtown, Uidh and Druimaphuinnd, and a new farm-house had been built on the south side of the hill, where the township fank is today. The present crofting township of Northton is built between the former villages of Uidh and Druimaphuinnd.

Ob   A village in South Harris, later the scene of Lord Leverhulme's fishery schemes, and renamed Leverburgh. From the Norse Hop, for a sheltered anchorage.

Old Castle   The ruins of the old castle of the MacLeods still stand on a knoll at the east point of Pabbay.

Pabbay   An island at the western end of the Sound of Harris. Once reckoned as the granary of Harris because of its fertility, it was cleared for sheep in 1842.

Peinn Domhnuill   A former village in Uig, Lewis, now part of the township of Ardroil.

Rodell   Rodel, the southmost village of Harris, built around the Church of St. Clement, and the harbours and houses erected in the 1780s by Captain Alexander MacLeod of Harris as part of his fisheries scheme.

Ronaval   Roneval, the highest hill in South Harris, above the village of Obbe, and at present under consideration as the site of a super-quarry.

Ru an Teampuill   The headland at the Teampull, which also contains the remains of an iron age broch.

Scaladil   A village on the west shore of Loch Seaforth, beside Ardvourlie Castle.

Scalpay   An island off the east coast of Harris. It is still a centre of the fishing industry, and is soon to be connected by bridge to mainland Harris.

Scarista   A group of two villages in west Harris, cleared for sheep in 1826.

Scarp   An island off the northwest point of Harris, which maintained a population until about twenty years ago.

Scianaid   A former village on the north shore of Loch Resort, between Torray and the mouth of the Loch.

Seilebost   A township in West Harris, cleared in 1838.

Shelay   Shillay - an island at the west end of the Sound of Harris, between Pabbay and Coppay.

Soay   A group of two islands sheltering the entrance to Loch Leosavay. They were tenanted along with the mainland opposite by MacAulays, and later crofted for short periods.

South Town   A former village on the west face of Toe Head, cleared to add to the farm of North Town for MacGillivray.

Sta   The beach below the present Borve Lodge, and the stream running into it.

Strond   A farm on the south coast of Harris, then occupied by Mrs Campbell.

Stron na Sguirt   Sron Scourst, a rock face above Glen Meavag.

Suiannebhal   A hill on the shore of Loch Suainavat in Uig.

Summit of Ben Luskentir (p52)   Not the top of the mountain itself, but the top of the pass at Beul na Bearnadh.

Tarbert   Now the capital of Harris, on the isthmus between East and West Lochs Tarbert, but then an insignificant village.

Tarcla   The cliff slopes of the northwest face of Ben Luskentyre, facing into West Loch Tarbert. A difficult and dangerous place to traverse.

Tastir   A hillslope between the North Town farmhouse and the entrance to South Town.

Temple   Teampull na h-Uidhe - the ruins of a sixteenth century chapel built by Alasdair Crotach at the same time as St Clement's at Rodel. It lies on a headland to the north of South Town.

Timsgarry   A township in the centre of the Parish of Uig, where John MacAskill taught school. The Church and Manse of Uig are also in this area.

Toray   A former village on the north shore of Loch Resort, about halfway between Kinloch Resort and its mouth.

Torgibost   Horgabost - one of the first townships in West Harris to be cleared for sheep. Resettled in the 1930s as a crofting township.

Traigh na Clibhadh   A beach on the western side of the Uidh, near to the entrance to South Town.

Traigh na h-Uidhe   The same beach as Mol na h-Uidhe, since at some tides the whole of the Mol is covered in sand.

Uadh Lot   The first word will be Uamh, a cave, and presumably it is on Pabbay, though the name is not now in use.

Ui   A former village on the machair of Northton. The word means isthmus, and is also applied to the whole machair area.

Urga   Urgha - a village between Tarbert and Scalpay. The old road to Stornoway led from Urgha through the hills to Maraig and the Lewis boundary.

Valamus   A former farm in the Pairc area of the district of South Lochs in Lewis.

Part 2 Persons

Aonas Mac Dhomhnuill 'ic Ioin bhan   Properly Aonghas mac Dhomhnaill mhic Iain Bhain - Angus son of Donald son of Fair John - shepherd for Luskentyre at Ceanndibig.

Aonas mac Uilliam   Properly Aonghas mac Uilleim - Angus son of William - not identified.

Armiger   Armiger Nicolson from Skye, schoolmaster in Strond, later referred to as "the Bishop".

Aunt Marcella from Glasgow   Sister of Roderick MacGillivray, otherwise unknown.

Ban gosti   Gaelic for "foster-mother" - presumably William's nurse in his earliest years in Harris.

Bethune Mr   Rev. Alexander Bethune, minister of Harris from 1806 to 1831. He was married to Isabella MacDonald, of Greshornish on Skye, with family Neil, William, Isabella, Helen, Donald and Janet. He occupied the farm of Big Borve in lieu of part of his stipend.

Bethune Miss Christina   Sister of Rev. Alexander Bethune.

Bethune Roderick   Son of John Bethune, joint tenant of Scarista, evicted in 1826.

Cameron Mr   Tutor to the Campbells of Strond and Killigray.

Campbell Archie   One of the Campbells of Strond and Killigray.

Campbell Donald, of Taransay   Son of Captain Kenneth Campbell of the Uidh in Taransay. Later killed in a brawl at Dunvegan Castle.

Campbell Mrs, of Killigray   Ann, wife of Kenneth Campbell of Strond and Killigray. She was the twenty-fifth child of Donald MacLeod of Berneray (- and not the youngest!)

Campbell Mrs, Scarista   Wife of Malcolm Campbell, joint tenant in Scarista, evicted in 1826.

Campbell Neil   Not identified - probably one of the Campbells of Strond and Killigray.

Car John   Not identified, but there were Kerrs still in Strond until recently.

Clark John   "married to a niece of my uncle's wife" i.e. Barbara, daughter of Murdo MacKenzie and Janet MacAskill.

Conith mac Ioin ic Dhomhnaill   Properly Coinneach mac Iain mhic Dhomhnaill - Kenneth son of John son of Donald - not identified.

Degraves Mr   It is known that MacLeod of Harris had a harbour-master and land overseer living at Rodel, and no doubt this is he.

Dingwall Mr, Uist   Presumably Alexander Dingwall, innkeeper at Kersavagh. Lochmaddy.

Domhnul Ban mac Thormid 'ic Ioin Bhain   Properly Domhnall Ban mac Thormoid mhic Iain Bhain - Fair Donald son of Norman son of fair John - not identified.

Donald my brother   William's step-brother, later tacksman of Eoligarry in Barra.

Each brogach   Gaelic for "the shod horse" - MacGillivray's favourite mount. (The other farm ponies would have been unshod).

Euphemia, my father's widow   The reason for MacGillivray's being sent to live with his uncle at North Town was his father's marriage to Effie MacNeil, daughter of William MacNeil of Pabbay. This phrasing, and the dispute about the lease of North Town, suggest that, by the end of the period of the journal, relations between the two branches of the family had deteriorated badly. It is interesting to note that, by 1830, neither MacGillivray nor his sister-in-law had North Town, which had been added to the farms of Alexander MacRa, cousin and colleague of Donald Stewart the factor!

Fear of Luskentyre   Donald Stewart's predecessor as "Fear" or tenant of Luskentyre was Isabella MacLeod, who was married to Dr William MacLeod of Glendale. She later removed to Luskentyre House, Stornoway.

Ferguson Alexander   Teacher in Pabbay, and father of family later at Sruparsaig, Geocrab.

Ferguson Donald   Not identified - presumably a tenant in Rodel.

Fraser Mr   Simon Fraser, Minister of Stornoway from 1815 to 1824, when he was drowned crossing the Minch (and the early Presbytery records were lost with him).

Gaelic Schoolmaster of Strond   Armiger Nicolson from Skye, later referred to as "the Bishop".

"Gentleman of Kintail"   Alexander MacRa of Hushinish, later tacksman of North Town and other extensive farms in Lewis and Harris.

Gosti   Gaelic for "Godfather", in this case, but can also mean foster-father.

Grant Mr, of Ulinish   Tacksman of Ullinish in Skye.

Harriet Miss   From the context, a sister of Miss Inglis and Mrs MacLeod of Harris.

Iain ma Dhomh'll ruaidh   Properly Ian mac Dhomhnaill Ruaidh - John son of Red Donald.

Iain mac Choinnich ic Iver   John son of Kenneth son of Evander - not identified.

Inglis Miss   Sister of Mrs Alexander Norman MacLeod of Harris.

Isabeil ni Challum ic Ailein   Isabella daughter of Malcolm son of Allan, presumably a servant at North Town.

MacAskill Mr, schoolmaster   John MacAskill, schoolmaster of Uig. He taught at Timsgarry in Uig for 26 years, before emigrating to Antigonish, Nova Scotia in 1819. He was married first to Christina Munro, with family Murdo, Janet, Catherine, Christina, John and Mary, and secondly to a Miss MacDonald, with family Helen and Marion.

MacAskill Marion   Step-sister of Mrs MacGillivray, she was later to be William's own wife.

MacAskill Mary   Mrs MacGillivray, the wife of William's uncle Roderick. She was a daughter of John MacAskill from Roag in Skye, schoolmaster in Uig, Lewis.

MacAskill Nelly   Full sister of Marion MacAskill, she emigrated with her father to Nova Scotia, where she later married Hugh MacDonald of Antigonish.

MacAskill of Ardhasig   John MacAskill, ground officer of North Harris.

MacCuish Donald   Shepherd at Druimaphuinnd, and later tenant at Strond, where descendants lived until recently.

MacDiarmid Ewen and wife Christina MacAskill   Ewen MacDiarmid was married to Christina MacAskill, sister of Mrs MacGillivray. He was employed for a time as shepherd at Luachair, but the family emigrated to Antigonish, Nova Scotia, in the 1820s.

MacDiarmid John, the merchant   Not identified, but there are still MacDermids in Harris whose origins were in Strond.

MacDonald Jessie of Ord   A cousin of Mrs MacGillivray - presumably through Mrs MacGillivray's grandmother who was a MacDonald.

MacDonald John, Scarista   Joint tenant in Scarista, evicted in 1826.

MacDonald John merchant   Not identified.

MacDonald Malcolm, of Rodel   Tenant of the kelp-shores of Lingerbay. He belonged to the Stalcairean MacDonalds who came to Harris from North Uist.

MacDonald Norman, from Uist   Not identified.

MacDonald Mr (p35)   Probably Kenneth MacDonald, joint tenant of Rodel.

MacFarlane Mr   Tutor to the Stewart children in Luskentyre.

MacGillivray Mr   Roderick MacGillivray, farmer of North Town, uncle of William MacGillivray.

MacGillivray Mrs, (of Pabbay)   Effie, daughter of William MacNeil of Pabbay, and wife of William MacGillivray senior.

MacGillivray William senior   Brother of Roderick MacGillivray of North Town

MacKay Angus, Glasgow   Married to Marion, sister of Roderick MacGillivray.

MacKenzie Donald   Not identified.

MacKenzie Kenneth, of Stornoway   The son of a ship-master in Stornoway.

MacKenzie William, from Tarbert   "Uilleam Ruadh" - Red William - fishcurer in Tarbert; married to Mary, sister of Murdo MacLellan of Scalpay and St. Kilda.

MacKinlay Dr   The local doctor in Harris - not otherwise identified.

MacLachlan Mr   Not identified.

MacLean the Schoolmaster   Not identified.

MacLellan Duncan, of Ensay   Brother of Murdo MacLellan of Scalpay and St. Kilda. Later tacksman of Habost, Lochs, Lewis.

MacLellan Murdoch   Son of Donald MacLellan of Taransay; tacksman of Scalpay, and later of St.Kilda. Married to Marion MacNeil of Pabbay, and their daughter Christina later married Donald MacGillivray of Eoligarry.

MacLennan Roderick, Scarista   Son of Angus MacLennan, joint tenant in Scarista, evicted in 1826.

MacLeod Dr   Dr William MacLeod, tacksman of Luskentyre before Donald Stewart.

MacLeod John - Iain ma Dhomh'll ruaidh   Properly Ian mac Dhomhnaill Ruaidh - John son of Red Donald - tenant in Rodel.

MacLeod John, Scarista   Joint tenant in Scarista, evicted in 1826.

MacLeod Kenneth   Joint tenant in Little Borve, evicted in 1838.

MacLeod Kenneth, from Taransay   Son-in-law of Kenneth Campbell of the Uidh on Taransay, later tacksman of Maraig.

MacLeod of MacLeod   MacLeod of Dunvegan, whose family formerly owned Harris also.

MacLeod the Laird   Alexander Norman MacLeod, grandson of Captain Alexander MacLeod of Berneray and Harris. In 1817 he married Richmond Inglis, and the marriage festivities of their tenants in Rodel are described later in the journal. Within a year, all the tenants were evicted from Rodel. By 1830 MacLeod was bankrupt, and Harris was sold in 1834 to Lord Dunmore.

MacLeod Mr   Tacksman of Maraig, and from the context a lay preacher in the Church in Harris. He lost the lease of Maraig in 1818 to Captain Kenneth Campbell. A John MacLeod is shown then as tenant of Island Seaforth, and perhaps this is he.

MacLeod Mr Lachlan   Minister of St Kilda from 1788-1830, succeeding his father there. Married Marion MacLean of Kinloch, Dunvegan, with family Angus, Donald, Norman, Flora, Roderick, Alexander and Roderick.

MacLeod Roderick   Presumably a son or brother of MacLeod of Maraig.

MacLeod Rory, of Craco   Roderick MacLeod, joint tenant of Crago - evicted in 1838.

MacMillan Marion   Not identified.

MacNabb Mr & Mrs   Duncan MacNab from Islay and his wife Peggy Campbell of Scalpay. They had emigrated to Carolina with her father, Donald Campbell of Scalpay, but returned after the American Revolutionary War. They later moved to Taransay, then to Kyles Scalpay.

MacNaughton Mrs   John MacNaughton was shepherd at Clettihog, on Little Loch Roag. His wife was Janet MacKinlay.

MacNeil of St Kilda   William MacNeil, tacksman of Pabbay and St. Kilda.

MacNeil Norman   Son of William MacNeil of Pabbay, and brother of William MacGillivray's stepmother. He was married to Mary MacKillop from Berneray, and they later emigrated to Mira, Cape Breton.

MacNeil Roderick, of Kyles   Son of William MacNeil, of Pabbay; tacksman of Kyles Berneray (Newton) in North Uist. Married to Isabella MacLean, with children Donald, Ewen, William and Mary.

MacPhaic John   MacPhaic is an old surname from the Island of Berneray, now usually translated as MacKillop - for no very good reason!

MacRa Alexander, of Hushinish   Later tacksman of North Town and extensive farms in Lewis and Harris.

MacRae Mr   William MacRae, Minister of Barvas from 1813 to 1856.

MacRae Mr Finlay   Minister of North Uist from 1815 to 1858, and tacksman of Vallay Island.

Mac Iain og mhic Cuthis   "a son of young John MacCuish" shepherd for North Town at Gob an Tobha - the Point of Toe Head.

Morrison Kenneth   Joint tenant in Borve Beag, evicted in 1838.

Munro Mr   Hugh Munro, Minister of Uig from 1774 to 1823. Married Janet, daughter of John MacAskill of Rhu an Dunan in Skye, with family Catherine, John, Christina and Marion.

Niall mac Thormid bhain   Properly Niall mac Thormoid Bhain - Neil son of Fair Norman - not identified.

Niall mac Thormid ic Neil   Neil son of Norman son of Neil. His grandfather Neil MacLeod, of the Albannaich family, was joint tenant of Seilebost, evicted in 1838.

Oibhrig nighean Ioin ghairbh   Properly Oighric nighean Iain Ghairbh - Effie, daughter of rough John.

Oona and Margaret, Misses   In Rev Simpson's household, and perhaps his sisters.

Robinson John   Collector of Customs in Stornoway.

Rory of Kinresort Roderick MacLennan, gamekeeper at Kinloch Resort.

Ross the catechist Perhaps Donald Ross of Gisla, who later emigrated to Cape Breton.

Ross Mr Excise Officer.

Shaw Miss Margaret Not identified.

Simson Mr Alexander Simpson, Minister of Lochs from 1793 to 1830. He married Janet Graham, with family Colin, John, Ann, George, Alexander (or Sandy), Charles, Janet and Jessie.

Sinclair Rob Not identified.

Stewart, Alexander and Archie Brothers of Donald Stewart in Luskentyre. Tenants of the sheep-farm of Pairc in Lewis, and responsible for the clearances in that area.

Stewart Donald Donald Stewart, tacksman of Luskentyre and factor of Harris. He married Isabella MacRae, with children Donald, William, Margaret, Robert, Alexander, Hannah, Richmond, John, Helen, Mary, Grace and Jessie. He gradually cleared all the arable areas of Harris to form sheep farms for himself and his cousin Alexander MacRa of Husinish.

Taithis Presumably meant for "taibhse", the Gaelic word for a spectre.

Tormod Ban of Torray Not identified.

Torrie Mr Alexander Torrie, from Argyll, farmer of Nisabost, the first part of South Harris to be cleared to make a sheep-farm. By 1822 he had removed to the tack of Gramisdale in Benbecula.

"Uncle Toby" A pet name for Roderick MacGillivray of North Town.

"a wright" "married to an elder sister of my uncle's wife" i.e. Murdo MacKenzie married to Janet MacAskill.

Family Tree No 1

Illustrating the inter-relationships between tacksman families in Harris

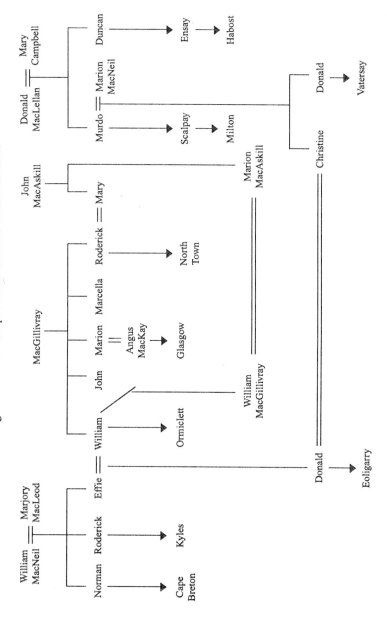

Family Tree No 2

Some of the descendants of John MacAskill, schoolmaster in Uig

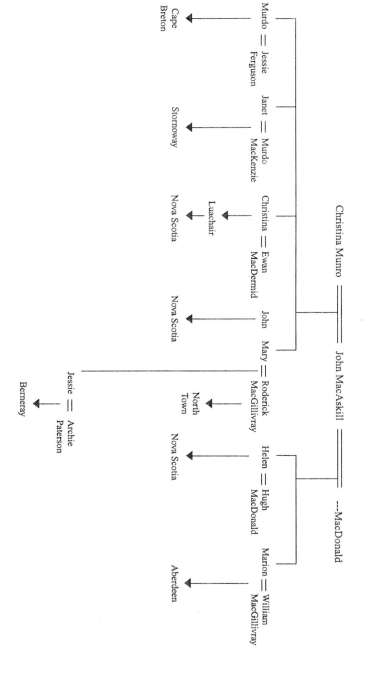

Christina Munro === John MacAskill === ---MacDonald

Murdo = Jessie Ferguson → Cape Breton

Janet = Murdo MacKenzie → Stornoway

Christina = Ewan MacDermid

Luachair → Nova Scotia

John → Nova Scotia

Mary = Roderick MacGillivray

North Town → Nova Scotia

Jessie = Archie Paterson → Berneray

Helen = Hugh MacDonald → Nova Scotia

Marion = William MacGillivray → Aberdeen